TRADITIONAL ART OF
AFRICA
OCEANIA
AND THE
AMERICAS

Jane Powell Dwyer
and
Edward Bridgman Dwyer

THE FINE ARTS MUSEUMS
OF SAN FRANCISCO

Copyright © 1973 by The Fine Arts Museums of San Francisco
Library of Congress Catalog Card Number: 73–75844
Designed and produced by Dave Comstock
Photographs by James Medley (unless otherwise noted)
Composed in Fairfield and Futura Black by Brekas Typesetting, Inc.
Printed by The Marier Engraving Company
on Warren's Cameo Dull White Paper
furnished by the Zellerbach Paper Company
Bound by Mountain States Bindery

THE FINE ARTS MUSEUMS
OF SAN FRANCISCO

EXHIBITED AT THE
M. H. DE YOUNG MEMORIAL MUSEUM

Foreword

The nucleus of the collection which is the basis for this book was assembled in the late 19th century. Among the earliest objects to come to the Museum, they are associated with the founding of the institution as part of the Mid-Winter Fair of 1894, which was a sequel organized by M. H. de Young, on a smaller scale, of the famous Columbian Exposition of 1893 in Chicago. The Mid-Winter Fair was the impetus not only for the founding of the M. H. de Young Memorial Museum but the development of Golden Gate Park.

The collection has grown over the years by donations and by selective purchases. It has not been on display for a number of years, but is once again finding a home in a newly renovated gallery devoted to the Traditional Arts of Africa, Oceania, and the Americas. There has been very limited opportunity for the museum-visiting public to see such a collection in Northern California. We hope that the presentation of this exciting material will stimulate further understanding and appreciation of cultures other than our own.

It was the de Young Museum Auxiliary who first saw the value of re-establishing a gallery devoted to the Traditional Art of Africa, Oceania, and the Americas and we are grateful to them for funds which provided for the vital preliminary work of research, cataloguing and conservation of the collection. Our thanks for further assistance in this work goes to the Mared Foundation, Mrs. Ralph Bennett, Amanda Hamilton, Jessie Jonas, Alice Gowanlock, Joseph M. Bransten, Robert Bransten, Mrs. Osborne White, W. S. Picher, and Mr. and Mrs. Gerald Wentling.

The construction of the gallery itself with a controlled environment for the objects has been possible due to generous grants from the National Endowment for the Arts, the Samuel H. Kress Foundation, The Hearst Foundation, and the Louis Lurie Foundation. We are deeply indebted to the individuals responsible for these foundations who understood the importance of this undertaking, as we are to our own de Young Museum Society and the Patrons of Art and Music who generously accepted not only the challenge to match these grants from their own membership funds, but to support the publication of this book as well. Special thanks goes to the Fireman's Fund American Foundation for the inclusion of an audio system.

A special note of appreciation to Jane Powell Dwyer, Director of the Haffenreffer Museum of Anthropology, Brown University, Providence, Rhode Island, and Edward Dwyer for their help in organizing the collection and the writing of this book.

The success of the project is attributable in many ways to the members of the staff who shared in its realization. Two in particular can be singled out. Royal A. Basich, Exhibition Designer, is largely responsible for the brilliant gallery design and installation. Thomas K. Seligman, Curator of the collection, not only grasped the cultural significance of the collection, but he immediately encouraged community participation in developing programs to utilize it. We shall be thanking him in the years to come for his wisdom as the gallery takes its rightful place as a community cultural resource.

IAN MCKIBBIN WHITE
Director of the Museums

Preface

Many people have generously given their time to assist in the preparation of this book. I wish to express gratitude to the Board of Trustees and to the Director of Museums, Ian White, who had the vision and interest to bring into being the gallery devoted to the Traditional Art of Africa, Oceania and the Americas for which this catalogue was written. Grateful acknowledgement is also made to the Museum's Docent Council and to the Patrons of Art and Music and The de Young Museum Society whose support and encouragement made this project possible. I would particularly like to thank Thomas Seligman, Curator of the collection, who coordinated and guided this volume to final production. Thanks are also, due to Sarah Gill, Judith Reis and Kathleen Berrin, and to the many other members of the Museum staff who contributed in different ways to help put this volume together. Appreciative acknowledgement is made to James Medley, Museum Photographer, whose excellent color and black and white photographs illustrate this volume.

Special thanks are due to Anna Bennett and Jessie Jonas who were enthusiastically involved with the project from the very beginning and to Bette Levin whose interest and hard work helped make this endeavor a success. Thanks also are expressed to Dr. William R. Bascom, Dr. James Bennyhoff, Dr. Karen O. Bruhns, Mr. Lawrence E. Dawson, Ms. Margaret Hoyt, Dr. Fritz Riddel, Mr. Norman Wilson and to the numerous other friends and colleagues who have offered their expertise and assistance.

JPD
Providence, Rhode Island 1973

AFRICA

Atlantic
Ocean

Mediterranean Sea

Red

S A H A R A

MALI

NIGER

CHAD

SENEGAL

Niger

River

GAMBIA

PORT GUINEA

Nalu
Baga

GUINEA

Bambara

Dogon

Bobo

Mossi

S
UPPER VOLTA

U

D

A

N

Lake Chad

Lobi

GHANA

Senufo

Temme
SIERRA LEONE Mende

Kissi

Kpelle

LIBERIA

Dan Guro Baule

Ngere

Bassa Kran

IVORY COAST

Bete

Ashanti

Anyi

TOGO

DAHOMEY

Yoruba

Ife

Benin City

NIGERIA

Ibo Ekoi

Ibibio

BaMun

Bamileke

CAMEROON

CENTRAL AFRICAN REPUBLIC

Gulf of Guinea

RIO MUNI

Fang

GABON

Mpongwe

BaLumbo

CONGO
(BRAZZAVILLE)

BaKota

BaTeke

Congo

River

ZAÏRE

CABINDA

Mayombe

BaKongo

BaSuku

BaYaka

BaPende

BaJokwe

BaKuba

BaSonge

BaLuba

ANGOLA

0   100 200 300 400 500 600 700 800
STATUTE MILES

dac

Introduction

To many people the art of black Africa is sculpture, painting and decorative ornament. Obviously, those arts best known to us are the objects—lasting and concrete—which can be exported, touched, displayed and admired for their intrinsic aesthetic qualities alone. But these plastic and graphic forms are only a small part of the complex artistic heritage of the peoples of this continent. In many African societies poetry, oration, music and dance are considered the highest embodiment of artistic expression. Sculpture or painting may serve as dramatic or beautiful supplements to these other forms of expression. Complex and richly diverse ceremonial "productions" involving many other kinds of creative activity often accompany the making and use of masks and sculptured figures. In a museum, we necessarily view these objects out of context. The existence of the color, sound, and movement which once enlivened them and made them very plausible should not be forgotten.

THE BEGINNINGS   Sculptured and painted forms are also the only ones which have been preserved to afford us some glimpse of the art of ancient African cultures. Lasting even beyond oral tradition and remembered histories, these objects have been unearthed by archaeologists or, in rare instances, they have been handed down for centuries as heirlooms of earlier lineages or once-powerful dynasties. Since wood and fiber decay rapidly, the majority of preserved pieces are made of clay, stone or metal.

Among the earliest examples of African art are paintings and engravings drawn on natural rock outcrops discovered in now desolate locations in the Sahara. These seem to be the work of nomadic pastoralists who occupied much of the region when it was not desert, but fertile and hospitable, perhaps as early as the fourth millennium B.C. In East, and especially South Africa, the other regions where this rock art is abundant, the technique has been continued until relatively recent times.

The known distribution of rock art does not tend to overlap the areas where three dimensional sculpture predominated. In these areas, primarily in West and Central Africa, early evidence for sculpture takes the form of terra cotta figures which have been recovered in archaeological sites from Chad and Nigeria westward to Mali. Most of these have been found in northern Nigeria and are of a distinctive style associated with the Nok culture, dated from about the 5th century B.C. to the 3rd century A.D. Recent excavations have shown that the Nok people were farmers and potters, and, perhaps significantly, that they had begun to utilize the technology of iron working. Excavations in their village sites revealed a variety of evidence for this early metallurgy including furnaces and slag heaps as well as iron tools.

The Nok artists most certainly worked with wood and it has been theorized that their very fine sculptural style had originally developed in that medium. But curiously, at this early time, the Nok artists began experimenting with clay to create powerful yet sensitively modelled human and animal figures. Some fragments recovered are from remarkably large terra cotta sculptures—some estimated to have been life size—which must have been exceedingly cumbersome to model and incredibly difficult to fire. Perhaps, for the Nok people, the medium of fired clay had some symbolic connection with iron working, both processes combining fire and earth to produce what might have seemed to be magical substances. Certain of the Nok figures appear to be highly stylized renderings of particular individuals, perhaps representations of the ancestors. As in later Nigerian kingdoms, where the ancestral images of the ruling groups were venerated, Nok figures probably had some significance in the political structure of the community. One may speculate that individuals who had mastered the new iron working technology—the blacksmiths—had powerful economic, political and military advantages over their neighbors. They may also have become religiously powerful figures in the community. Perhaps the Nok sculptures represent some aspect of the ritual and ceremony of this elite group.

In more recent times, metal and metal working were closely associated with the royal court in a number of West African kingdoms. At Ife in western Nigeria, for example, the god of iron was patron and protector of the royal family. Oral history and archaeological exploration reveal that the city of Ife was the religious and political capital of the early Yoruba and that it thrived from about the 8th century A.D.—perhaps earlier—to about the 15th century A.D. There are certain resemblances in the art of Ife to the Nok style, and it is often said that the people of Ife were the inheritors of the artistic traditions of the earlier Nigerian culture. In the Ife style, the predominant iconographic forms are delicately rendered portrait heads and full figures representing what apear to be royal personnages and attendants. Although their terra cotta and stone sculptures may have greater antiquity, the climax of Ife style is represented by exquisitely cast bronzes or brasses some of which date from the 11th

SOAPSTONE *POMDO* FIGURE. Kissi, Sierra Leone. 6″
x 2″; de Young Art Trust; #71.8.3.

TERRA COTTA COMMEMORATIVE HEAD. Kwahu,
Ivory Coast and Ghana. 16½″ x 8½″; Gift of Mrs. T. E.
Hanley; #60.30.1.

century A.D. Historical sources indicate that about 1400 A.D., perhaps earlier, the art of lost wax casting was introduced to Benin, a neighboring city state, by smiths from Ife. Shortly after this introduction, Ife lost its pre-eminence in metalworking.

Benin bronzes are among the best known examples of the African metal worker's skill and artistry. The bronzesmiths belonged to an honored guild which was part of the king's court and they lived and worked in a special ward within the walled city of Benin. They were entrusted with the manufacture of ritual objects for the shrines of the king's ancestors, the relief plaques and other ornaments used to decorate the palace and the insignia and emblems of the nobility. Benin's royal art tradition continued until the end of the 19th century when the city was attacked and destroyed by a British expeditionary force.

There are other West and Central African art styles for which there is some early history—although in antiquity they are not comparable to Nok or even Ife. Certain types of stone sculptures—usually carved of steatite—found from southern Sierra Leone eastwards to southern Guinea, are in this category. In Sierra Leone these are known as *nomoli* and some bear striking resemblances to documented 16th century ivory carvings of the coastal Sherbro people. The chronicles of early travelers in this region describe "statues of stone with which, they say, the people commune by incantation." This centuries old convention of carving small, grotesque human and animal figures continued with considerable vigor until quite recently. The Kissi of southern Guinea call these stone sculptures *pomdo,* a word associated with death and supernatural ancestral beings, and it is likely that both the *nomoli* and *pomdo* were originally ancestor figures. They have not yet been found in clear archaeological contexts, but instead, are usually unearthed by farmers in their fields or found with stone cutters' debris in caves or rock chambers along the veins of worked out steatite.

Clay sculptures made by the Ashanti of southern Ghana and by the Kwahu, a related people of the Ivory Coast, are also difficult to date. The idea of modelling clay heads, busts and full figures for use as commemorative or funerary monuments seems to have some antiquity but the practice was maintained up to recent times. Excavated sculptures dated to the 16th and 17th centuries have the distinctive characteristics of flattened, disc-like cranium and highly stylized facial features as do more modern examples. There are several other styles such as the Dogon *tellem* figures and certain types of

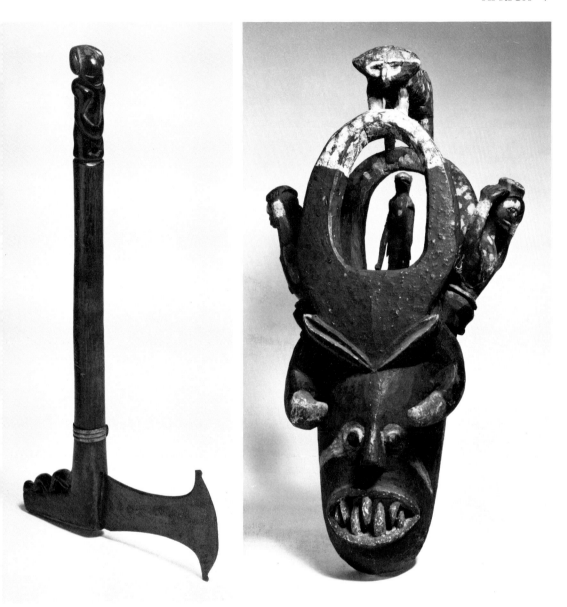

CEREMONIAL AXE. BaJokwe, Angola. 15″ x 5″; Bequest of Mr. Axel Peterson; #57.13.24.

MAUNG MASK. Ibo, Nigeria. 35½″ x 12½″; de Young Art Trust; #71.8.1.

BaKuba and BaKongo sculptures which may go back in time several centuries, but a great deal more archaeological work must be done before more than the sketchy outlines of African art history can be drawn. Evidence that this history is perhaps even more complex than we suspect is provided by the incredible diversity of 19th and 20th century African art styles and forms.

RECENT AFRICAN ART   The study of African art and what we know of its function has provided some insights into the reasons for artistic creativity and the diverse needs art satisfies in human society. Clearly, art is not only created to please man's sense of beauty, elegance or decoration, although this plays a very important part. Art not only gives pleasure but it gives power. Perhaps from their very beginnings, the plastic and graphic forms of art have been used as a means to bring the supernatural into view, to quell the fear of death and the unknown, to foretell the future and to transform and transcend everyday experience. The creation of art is one of man's ways of dealing with the imagined universe of the supernatural.

Art was also an instrument of power in the real world of individual status and political and social control. The sovereignty of kings or the authority of village headmen were displayed and enhanced in art forms symbolic of office. Among the BaJokwe, for example, axes and adzes with finely sculptured handles were not actually functional tools but served as the chief's insignia. In many African societies (as elsewhere in the world) art was also used to mark the male domain to the exclusion of women and to maintain male control over ritual. Women were seldom allowed to create ritual art. In many instances, they were not even allowed to see it, and were terrified by the men's tales of supernatural wrath or, more likely, fearful of punishment or even death if they should come in contact with the forbidden objects.

Some works of art had instilled in them the power to protect, some had the power to harm. Many kinds were made to recreate or recall dramatic myth or were used to present visual lessons of morality. Art was also made to observe the rites of passage, especially puberty ceremonies marking a young person's achievement of adult status, and funeral rites, which honored the transformation of the older individual into an ancestral spirit. Among the BaKwese, a small central Congo group, masks were worn by young men celebrating their triumphant return to the village after their initiation ordeal. The art made for these occasions is often brilliant and spectacular, created for display and to awe and to astonish the audience.

FEMALE PORTRAIT MASK. Ogowe River Area, Gabon.
11¼″ x 7½″; de Young Art Trust; #71.25.

FIBER HELMET MASK. BaKwese, Zaïre. 12¾″ x 11″;
Bequest of Mr. Axel Peterson; #57.13.4.

FEMALE ANCESTOR FIGURE. Bambara, Mali. 24″ x 8⅛″; Gift of Mrs. T. E. Hanley; #69.30.4.

ANTELOPE HEADDRESS (*chi wara* society). Bambara, Mali. 17¾″ x 4½″; Gift of Mr. and Mrs. Paul Breslow; #71.30.1.

Bambara

The western Sudan—now the republics of Mali and Upper Volta—is a region of dry savannah extending along the southern rim of the Sahara. It is the country of the Bambara, the Dogon, the Bobo, the Mossi and other smaller groups whose art belongs to the general category defined as the Sudanese style. Except in those areas where tribal boundaries meet and styles tend to mingle, each of these different peoples have their own distinctive art forms. But when viewed as a whole they share a number of very broad characteristics which set the art of the Sudan apart from that of adjacent areas. These styles tend toward geometrization of forms, emphasis on straight, linear elements rather than on rounded, curvilinear volumes, and elaborate surface decoration of incised or painted patterns.

These are very broad generalizations, however, and within each tribal style—even within the style of each sub-group—there is evident wide variation and modification. The magnitude of such variation has only recently been recognized. There is regional diversity to be sure but wide style variation can be found even within a single community, based upon widely divergent functions of different categories of objects or in other cases because of the artist's use of different materials requiring different techniques, or even due to the fact that different groups of artists make each category of object.

The sculptural forms of the Bambara, for example, do not present an altogether unified style. The Bambara, who live along the lower reaches of the Niger River in Mali, are widely known for their extremely graceful carvings of antelopes. But they also have a wide range of other important and elegant sculptural forms, including a variety of masks, ancestor and fertility figures, altars, fetishes or power figures, puppets and musical instruments which are less familiar to western eyes. Much of this art was created for use in the rituals of several interconnected and complex secret or graded societies. These societies, to which every male belonged, were the educational institutions, the work force and the controlling authority of the community.

Within the series of graded societies a man would pass through in his lifetime, the first was the *N'tomo,* a form of primary school for the very young boys. The next step was the *Chiwara* society whose members were the young men who did most of the heavy agricultural work. The antelope figure which was attached to a basketry cap and worn by a dancer was the primary motif of this grade. It portrayed a mythological being, half man, half antelope who, according to Bambara belief, taught mankind the arts of cultivation. This legendary being is believed incarnate in the wearers of the antelope head-dresses which at planting and harvest festivals appeared in pairs—a male and a female—to symbolically insure the fertility of the earth.

Mature men make up the membership of other societies such as the *Komo* whose sacred cult objects are remarkably different in form, style and manufacture from those of the *N'tomo* and *Chiwara* ranks. The *Komo* society was associated with the blacksmith and participants in its rites were believed to be the embodiment of the primordial blacksmith, considered as the original source of all human knowledge and skills.

Senufo
The Senufo wood carver was also the blacksmith, a fact noted among several other West African peoples, and it is significant that this artist-smith was regarded by the other members of Senufo society with some ambivilance. Because of his power to work fire and earth into metal, he was feared but yet respected. He made the tools, weapons and the sacred and magical paraphernalia of ritual essential to the community, but he lived apart from the village, belonging to a caste segregated from the tribal group.

The art of the Senufo who lived in Mali, Upper Volta and in the northern districts of the Ivory Coast, has often been said to constitute a transition between the geometric tendencies of the western Sudanese styles and the more naturalistic, curvilinear emphasis found in the southern Ivory Coast and neighboring regions to the east.

An important class of Senufo carving is the ancestor figure. These sculptures, representing both male and female human figures, were made to symbolize, portray, honor, commemorate and even to provide a temporary abode for the souls of the dead. If accorded sufficient attention and respect, ancestral souls were believed to protect the living and to act as intermediaries between man and the more remote gods or forces of the supernatural. The concept of ancestor spirits as transcendent beings which could be honored and persuaded by prayer or sacrifice to come to man's material or spiritual aid can perhaps in some ways be compared to the Christian idea of saints. The ancestors were not thought of as gods, but certainly having more spiritual power than mere living mortals, they served to bring the essence of the supreme god or the higher deities closer to humanity.

FEMALE ANCESTOR FIGURE. Senufo, Central Ivory
Coast. 14″ x 4½″; Lent Anonymously; #L71.12.6.

MOTHER OF THE PORO SOCIETY. Gio (Dan), Liberia.
17½″ x 5⅛″; de Young Art Trust; #71.26.

Dan-Ngere, Mende, Loma

The idea that power resides in a work of art is brought out with great clarity in the study of the secret society masks of the Mende, Loma and the different peoples of the large Dan-Ngere complex. The Mende name *Poro* is given to this society which is of the utmost importance in Sierra Leone, Guinea and Liberia. Since one of the main ritual items used by the society is the mask, so called *Poro* masks are predominant in collections of sculpture from these areas of West Africa.

The *Poro* was an all inclusive male society which functioned to initiate young men in the social, religious and professional roles they would fulfill as adults and to control the behavior of all members of the community. There was also a female counterpart, called the *Sande* or *Bundu* society which taught young girls their duties as wives and mothers. In the past, the process of initiation into the *Poro* society consisted of a three or four year school, secluded and secreted in the bush where boys were instructed by important leaders called *zos*. During this period they learned a certain amount of secret ritual, were subjected to severe discipline—death for disclosing a *Poro* secret—and ultimately, were transformed into adult members of the community.

Within the *Poro* there were various levels. Even after his return from the bush school an individual could advance himself by payment of fees and by learning more ritual knowledge. There is some evidence to suggest that the higher ranks were hereditary, but because of the very secret nature of the organization it is more difficult to learn about this inner circle. Every important member of the *Poro* society had a small "portrait" mask just big enough to fit in the palm of his hand. This mask, called *ma,* which perhaps represented the soul of its owner, was prayed to and periodic sacrifices were made to it. A larger mask was the *ma* of the *Poro* society and it was kept inside a sacred enclosure during ceremonies. Members swore on this mask that they had abstained from sexual activity and had brought no evil intentions into the *Poro* area.

There were many other specific kinds of masks which were owned or cared for by *Poro* members. Naturally, more powerful masks were owned by more important persons within the society. These masks had many functions, but perhaps the most important ones involved the maintenance of social control. Masks were present at public functions and life-crisis ceremonies. The human manipulation of these masks was regulated and the power of decision and action was considered to reside within the mask rather than in the owner or operator. In this way the mask itself would assume the responsibility

BUNDU INITIATION MASK. Mende, Sierra Leone. 16″ x 8¼″; Lent by Mr. and Mrs. Henry Lutzky; #L71.26.1.

for its actions or decisions of serious consequence rather than the individual wearing it. If the wearer of a mask died, his place was taken by another so that the mask would continue to function. Generally, masks were called upon to settle disputes within the tribe and acted to control warfare between groups. They protected the individual against witchcraft and disease and insured the success of the harvest. Finally, they controlled the social ranking and advancement within the tribe and the *Poro* society itself.

BUSH SPIRIT MASK. Kran or Bete, Liberia or Ivory Coast. 12″ x 11½″; Gift of Mr. and Mrs. Paul Breslow; #71.30.2.

PORO SOCIETY MASK. Loma, Liberia. 34″ x 16½″; de Young Art Trust; #71.27.

MA GE MASK. Bassa, Liberia. 8½″ x 6¼″; Gift of the Links Group. #71.21.

Yoruba

The Yoruba are a very numerous and highly urbanized people in western Nigeria and eastern Dahomey. They are the descendants of Ife and their art suggests the inheritance of many elements from this classic African aesthetic and perhaps, even from the ancient art of Nok. Yoruba sculpture emphasizes a stylized naturalism and an interest in the portrayal of the human figure in life-like poses or attitudes. The Yoruba

MASKED ENTERTAINER (*Ge*). Loma, Sucramo, Liberia.
Photo by T. K. Seligman.

GELEDE SOCIETY MASK. Yoruba, Nigeria. 19½″ x 10″; de
Young Art Trust; #71.20.

GROUP OF *IBEJI* FIGURES. Yoruba, Nigeria. 7″ to 10″; Lent
Anonymously; #L71.12.50–59.

artist is also a colorist and characteristically will apply a range of bright commercial paints, even laundry bluing, as well as natural pigments whenever possible within the cannons of this style.

The Yoruba have a highly complex system of religious beliefs which include a vast pantheon of *orishas* or deities, each of which has its separate cult, particular ritual appurtenances and shrine furniture. The art made for the celebrations of certain of these cults allowed considerable innovation as, for example, in the complicated superstructures on many masks belonging to *gelede* society where novelty seems to have increased the mask's effectiveness. Members of this society, wearing these colorful masks, dance to propitiate and placate witches by entertaining them. The mask was brightly painted and frequently fitted with moving parts or added materials such as palm fronds and cloth to increase its descriptive or narrative quality and of course, its entertainment value.

On the other hand, sculpture associated with other cults might be far more conventional in form as are the characteristic *ibeji* or twin figures. The Yoruba believed twins to be sacred. If one or both of the twins should die, one or a pair of *ibeji* figures was carved, dressed, fed and cared for as if it were the living child, apparently in an attempt to induce the soul of the deceased infant to return to its family.

Cameroon

Perhaps the most elegant and luxurious of African art objects were made for kingly rulers and belong to the tradition of royal or courtly art. This tradition was developed among a number of widely distant peoples including the Ashanti of Ghana, the Fon of Dahomey, the BaMum of the Cameroon grasslands, in the Benin Kingdom of Nigeria and among the BaKongo and BaKuba of the Congo. The significant features of this art of the ruling classes differ markedly from what may be termed the more popular or folk arts.

The focus of the royal art styles is the king or exalted chief who is held to be divine by his subjects. This divinity derived from the ruler's claim to direct descent from the gods and served to instill into his person great spiritual as well as political power. In the localities where divine kingship held sway, earlier patterns of ancestor worship were usually modified and the king's ancestors usually took the place of local and family ancestral beings.

Royal art was created to glorify the king and the court nobility or the members of the upper classes, to help maintain their sovereign power and to surround them with symbolic, ceremonial and luxurious objects befitting and indicative of their status. Royal art styles tended to emphasize more naturalistic forms or, at least, idealized forms. The king would be portrayed in all his finery and ornate richness and shown with smaller attendant figures posed in attitudes of respect. Another frequent device was to depict the royal personnages together with the elaborate symbolism of the ruling lineage.

Certain prestige materials were reserved for the king's use alone or for those whom he chose to honor. Among such materials reserved as the royal prerogative were ivory, gold and certain other metals, cowrie shells and imported beads. Glass beads and cowries were an important means of exchange in many regions of Africa and, especially in the Cameroon, they were incorporated into the art and costume of the nobility as a symbol of wealth and prestige.

The Cameroon was a rich art producing area with great complexity of regional and tribal styles. The art of the peoples of the coast and western rain forests is poorly known, since many of their artistic activities ceased about the turn of the century when this area came under the influence of European commercial interests. In the south, there are indications in the art of relationships with the cultures of the Gabon. In the north, naturalistic, sometimes grotesque skin-covered masks and headdresses characteristic of that area are related to similar forms found among the better known Nigerian Ekoi.

Inland to the east, the terrain rises to a high fertile plateau known as the Cameroon grasslands. In the past, the region was divided into numerous small political entities ruled by feudal lords or kings. Much of the art of the grasslands region belonged to the royal or courtly artistic tradition. Among the BaMum, for example, the kings were the principal patrons of the local artists. The famous king Njoya who ruled about the turn of the century, maintained several museums in his capital city of Foumban. One of the characteristics of BaMum art, particularly that made for royalty, is sculpture covered with colorful beadwork. This is a complicated decorative technique in which a carved wooden base is first fitted with a layer of cloth, then on the cloth are sewn the shell and different colored glass beads.

CLAY PIPE BOWL. Grassland Area, Cameroon. 4⅛″ x 1″;
Gift of the Henry Crocker Estate; #59.12.10.

BEADED HEADDRESS. BaMum, Cameroon (collected before 1900). 9″ x 26″; de Young Art Trust; #71.15.

PAINTED FACE MASK. Fang (BaVuvi group), Gabon. 7¼″ x 6½″; Gift of Mr. and Mrs. Paul Breslow; #71.30.3.

Fang Among the first examples of African sculpture to attract the attention of European artists in the early 20th century were the masks and figures of the central African Fang. The influence of this style can be seen in the work of Amedeo Modigliani, it is perhaps also visible in Picasso's early Cubist paintings and it served as inspiration for the Fauvist artists André Derain, Maurice Vlaminck and Henri Matisse. In fact, a white faced Fang mask which belonged to Derain and is still in the collection of his descendants, was purchased in 1905 from Vlaminck. The latter is often credited with having been among the earliest of the modern western artists to "discover" African art.

The Fang are a complex group composed of numerous smaller tribal units who live along the coast from southern Cameroon and Rio Muni to Gabon. They are relatively recent migrants to this part of central Africa, for, according to documentary sources, they reached this area only a century or two ago. The original homeland of the Fang or Pahouin, as they are sometimes called, is not known exactly but stylistic features of their art point to a possible relationship with the Azande and other peoples of the northeastern Congo.

The Fang were a fierce and warlike people. Their vitality is mirrored in their sculpture which is among the most elegant from central Africa. Unlike many other African regional or tribal styles, Fang sculpture is limited to a relatively few forms, primarily reliquary figures and several types of masks. The reliquaries, darkly polished and serenely composed, are the best known of Fang sculpture. These were carved for the *bieri* cult which focused upon the veneration of the skulls and other remains of clan ancestors. Ancestral bones, kept in a cylindrical bark container, were guarded by the supernatural protective force of the *bieri* figure which was mounted on the container above them. Possession of these relics legitimized and guaranteed the status of pre-eminent clans.

Masks belonging to the Fang are somewhat rarer than the reliquary figures and they are stylistically quite different. As is fairly common in this region, the majority of masks are white faced, and, on many examples, simple contrasting detail is emphasized with red or black pigment. Many of the

NGI SOCIETY HELMET MASK. Fang, Gabon (collected before 1900). 19½″ x 11″; Gift of Mr. Siegfried Aram; #X71.7.

masks carved in the shape of elongated human faces belonged to an important cult group called the *ngi* society. According to early ethnographic sources, the function of the *ngi* society was to maintain peace and order within the community and to unify the numerous and diverse clan groups within the tribe. The society also served to protect its members from sorcery and witchcraft which were the cause of considerable anxiety among the Fang. Called upon when real or supernatural trouble struck a village, the masked leader of the cult could divine the cause of sickness and death, pointing out an individual guilty of sorcery or other criminal action. He could also call upon men of certain ranks in the society to punish the offender.

BaKongo

Another great art producing region of Africa is the Congo, a vast belt of dense tropical forest, stretching almost three quarters of the distance across the equatorial zone of the African continent. The area is crossed by numerous major rivers and their tributaries which serve as important routes of communication. Archaeologists have only recently begun to delve into the Congo's remote past and present evidence indicates that its first known inhabitants were related, or culturally and physically similar, to the present day Pygmies who still hunt and fish for their livelihood in the Congolese forests. By the beginning of the Christian era, perhaps earlier, BaNtu migrants gradually moved into the Congo bringing with them knowledge of metal smithing and agriculture. By 1000 A.D. at the latest, they had pushed the original Pygmy bands into refuge areas and had spread their more sophisticated way of life throughout the entire Congo region.

From about 1200 A.D. on, a number of powerful kingdoms arose in this region. One of the most celebrated was the Kingdom of the Kongo with its center located near the mouth of the Congo River. This realm was at the height of its power when the first Portuguese explorers reached the area, late in the 15th century. The Portuguese managed to convert the king and some of his subjects to Catholicism and to instill in them a taste for the imported luxuries of Europe. Although this religious conversion was short lived, the later figure sculpture of the BaKongo, unlike other Congolese styles, exhibits a remarkable degree of naturalism and may even attempt to indicate movement in gesture and body pose, features which may have developed during the period of early contact with the Europeans.

FETISH OR POWER FIGURE.
BaKongo, Zaïre (collected before
1900). 7¾″ x 3½″; Gift of the
Henry Crocker Estate; #59.12.11.

BaKuba

The BaKuba or Bushongo were a confederation of a number of tribes which in the 17th century formed a strong centralized state with a feudal system of government. The state was united under the leadership of the BaMbola group whose chiefs achieved royal or kingly status and enshrined their ancestors as deities.

BaKuba royalty differed little from other royal African traditions. The king was considered divine—the earthly descendant and representative of the creator god. He was surrounded by artistic symbols of his great power and by luxuries made by craft guilds attached to the court. His court was made up of a hierarchy of chiefly nobility and functionaries whose duty it was to maintain the glory of the king. Among these functionaries was the royal historian who was required to remember and transmit the tribal history and genealogy of the ruling lineage as it was traced, generation by generation, from the time

GARI MAASHI POLICE MASK. BaKuba, Zaïre. 10″ x 11″; de Young Art Trust; #72.3.1.

RAFFIA PILE CLOTH. BaKuba, Zaïre. 21″ x 17½″; Gift of Mrs. Gustave Brenner, 1931; #53809A.

WEDDING CUP. BaKuba, Zaïre. 10¾″ x 3″; Gift of the
Henry Crocker Estate; #59.12.13.

of creation. Although the events and individuals of the earliest generations were mythical, the accounts of later BaKuba kings appear to have been based on actual history. Each successive king was remembered for his exploits in war or for the benefits he brought to the community in peace.

One of the most beloved of these early rulers was Shamba Bolongongo, the 93rd king who lived about 1600 A.D. Shamba is remembered as a great patron of the arts who allowed the first representatives of the craft guilds into his court, and introduced various craft innovations such as weaving of raffia cloth and the art of embroidery.

The BaKuba excel in the manufacture of these embroidered textiles or "velvets." The men, who are the skilled and traditional weavers, make the base fabric, but the women apply the embroidery. BaKuba art is, in this aspect, unusual in that there is a close correspondence between patterns used by the women for these embroideries and those employed by the men to decorate carved wood objects such as boxes and palm wine cups and other functional items.

BaPende and BaSuku

In many regions of the world, an important reason for the creation of art is to mark specific significant points of an individual's passage through life. Birth, puberty, marriage and death are such primary occasions solemnified by ritual and celebrated in art. In Africa, ritual focus was upon puberty rites or the individual's entrance into adulthood and upon death, when he entered the realm of the ancestors. At the time of such changes in status, the community would ritually invoke the presence of the supernatural and participants would transform themselves with masks and costume, altering their ordinary patterns of movement and speech with dance and song to become one with the supernatural. Among the most varied and colorful masking forms were those created for the arduous process of initiation.

Initiation, almost universally, is considered to be the symbolic death of the novice and his rebirth as a fully statused member of the society. It was primarily an educational procedure but often the older members of the society administering and overseeing the rites would transform themselves into unearthly supernatural beings to terrify the youths into submission and obedience. For their part, the youths were usually required to alter their appearance by donning different types of masks and accompanying costume to denote

HEMBE INITIATION MASK.
BaSuku, Zaïre. 15″ x 11½″; Bequest of Mr. Axel Peterson;
#57.13.2.

HEMBE INITIATION
MASK. BaSuku, Zaïre. 18″ x
14½″; Bequest of Mr. Axel
Peterson; #57.13.1.

successful passage through the different states of their initiation. Often, the most striking or remarkable masks were worn by the initiates after completion of the ordeals and upon their triumphant return to the village.

A number of groups living in the districts of the Kwango and Kasai rivers in southwestern Zaïre—particularly the BaPende, BaYaka, BaSuku and BaJokwe—created a series of elaborate masks in conjunction with initiation into the *mukanda* or men's secret society. A major spiritual function of the society was to honor the ancestors by admitting new members who, with initiation, would be eligible themselves to take on the ultimate status of ancestor. These initiation rites were expensive to the villagers but it was thought that by neglecting such periodic infusion of new members, the ancestors would become angry.

Among the BaPende, there were two types of initiation masks, one type more sacred than the other. The ancestors were reincarnated in the sacred masks which were worn by the leaders and police presiding over the initiation. These masks, shaped of both wood or basketry, were grotesque and fearful in order to instill awe and respect into the minds of the young novices.

MBUYA DRAMATIC MASK. BaPende, Zaïre. 12″ x 9″; Bequest of Mr. Axel Peterson; #57.13.5.

They were closely associated with concepts of the ancestors and could not be seen by other than initiates on pain of death.

In this southwestern area, the use of the second type of less sacred mask for entertainment was widespread. The dramatic performances and the disguises employed were of a more secular character when compared to the proceedings and paraphernalia of the initiation. Among such groups as the Ba-Yaka and BaSuku, it was the initiates who undertook to stage the performances. After their return from the seclusion of the initiation they would spend several months traveling from village to village in the surrounding countryside to present these masked dramas. The masks worn were designed to attract the admiration of the audience, and were both naturalistic and fantastic in form, usually brightly painted and delicately shaped. Because originality of form and elaborateness of decoration were everywhere highly admired qualities, innovations in style and form among these dramatic masks were spread quickly from one locality to another.

Among the BaPende, usage of these masks for public entertainment became increasingly more secular, and the participants—the actors and dancers—would often be able to earn a living by performing. The maskers would pantomime scenes of comic or moral tone and mimic village characters. Although only four or five different masks would customarily appear in a single performance, there were many types of masks in use by BaPende, each apparently representing a different character. Although the specific identities of only a few masks have been recorded, they seem to have been caricatures of local village types such as the old man, the vain dandy, the widow, the coquette and finally, the clown or fool who usually introduced the performance.

These masks are delicately carved with the high rounded forehead and snub nose characteristic of BaPende style. The eye which is slit and heavy and the sensitively carved mouth are exceedingly expressive of what might have been meant to be anger, contentment, pride, self satisfaction, hostility and other emotions. These expressive features are painted red with details and patterning highlighted in white and black, and the face is set off with quite naturalistic forms of hair and headdress woven or plaited in dark raffia.

MBUYA DRAMATIC MASK. BaPende, Zaïre. 22½″ x 8″;
Bequest of Mr. Axel Peterson; #57.13.7.

BaJokwe

The BaJokwe are among the largest of central Africa's tribal groups. Today, they are fighting Portuguese colonial rule, but in the 18th and 19th centuries they participated in the slave trade, prospered and grew into an aggressive political force, spreading throughout southwestern Zaïre, northern Angola and east into Zambia. Since the BaJokwe have long maintained trade connections with Europe, some of their art forms show direct foreign influence as in the European shape of the typical chief's chair. However, the style of the chair's unusual ornamentation—the three dimensional human and animal figures—is purely BaJokwe. The central motif is that of a human head which is shown wearing the elaborate headdress mask known as the "chief of the earth," a feared and revered supernatural considered to be the embodiment of power and fertility. This mask is characterized by great loops at the sides of the head. It is worn by the important tribal elder who is the leader of the initiation rites.

Female figures used as decorative designs are also typical of this style

CHIEF'S CHAIR. BaJokwe, Angola. 21″ x 10½″; Bequest of Mr. Axel Peterson; #57.13.18.

SNUFF MORTAR. BaJokwe, Angola. 9¼″ x 2″; Gift of
the Henry Crocker Estate; #59.12.8.

FETISH OR POWER FIGURE. BaYaka, Zaïre. 8¼″ x 3″;
de Young Art Trust; #72.3.2.

and in many cases may have been intended to represent female spirits—in actuality always impersonated by male dancers wearing female masks. The female mask or *mwana po* is a protective device and one of the finest and best known forms of BaJokwe art. It is said that the sculptor usually modelled the face of this mask as a stylized portrait of the most beautiful woman in the village and included many naturalistic elements such as specific patterns of facial scarification and hair dress in his design.

BaYaka, BaSonge

Belief in witchcraft and sorcery was a significant social and psychological phenomenon in many parts of the Congo and was the basis for the creation of a variety of sculptures which acted as protective devices against such malevolence. These are known as fetishes or power figures.

A fetish is, by definition, a manufactured object thought to contain within it some kind of supernatural force. This force can be dominated by the maker of the fetish or by someone equally knowledgeable in the particular esoteric wisdom of its control. Such fetishes were not usually objects of religious worship. Magical substances were inserted into cavities in the figure's stomach or head, hung from the neck and waist or formed into a ball of organic materials encasing the body of the sculpture. The carver would take the functional aspect of the power figure into consideration and would balance the crowded or bulging shape of the magical substances with sturdy lower limbs or enlarged head or headdress.

The BaYaka who live in the region of the Kwango River in western Zaïre make a distinctive type of fetish figure, carved with a pronounced aquiline or up-turned nose. Since the power of these fetishes was thought to derive from substances wrapped around the figure, the body or torso was spare and narrow, and details indicated schematically or not at all. Huge wedge-shaped feet, another characteristic BaYaka feature, were added to stabilize the heavily laden figure. Such fetishes were of considerable importance to the BaYaka. They were thought to belong to the ancestors, some engendering the magic necessary for successful hunting while others presided over the proceedings of initiation.

In the Kasai-Katanga district in eastern Zaïre, associations or societies formed around particular fetishes which were believed to be extraordinarily efficacious. In fact, membership in some of these associations grew so large

FETISH OR POWER FIGURE. BaSonge, Zaïre (collected before 1900). 24″ x 5″; de Young Art Trust; #71.16.

that the group was also able to wield considerable political power. Among these groups, misfortune, sickness and death were not natural occurrences but were caused by the sinister magic of some dissatisfied, revengeful or jealous individual. This anxious preoccupation with sorcery was eased by the activities of the fetisher or curer who would call upon the protective energy of his power figures to guard against such evil and misfortune.

Among the most elaborate of these fetish figures and sometimes, although rarely, among the most beautiful, were made by the BaSonge. In this style, the cranium was typically enlarged and possibly hollowed out to hold the magical potion or the stomach might be similarly filled. To add to their potency, these figures were covered with packets of magic powders and other substances, charms and medicines of all kinds, usually hiding all but the elegant elongated neck and sensitively sculptured head.

OCEANIA

Philippine
Sea

North

Philippines

Mariana Islands   MICRONESIA

Yap Islands   Marshall Islands

Palau   Truk Islands
Islands
          Caroline Islands

                                                          Gilbert Islands

Geelvink   Admiralty Islands
Bay   New Ireland
Sepik River   Bougainville   MELANESIA
New Guinea   New Britain   Solomon Islands
          Gulf
          of Papua   Massim   Santa Cruz Islands

                                                          New   Fiji Islands   Samoa
                                          Malekula   Hebrides   Island
                                                          Islands

                                                                                        Tong
                                                                                        Island
                              New Caledonia

AUSTRALIA

                              Tasman

                              Sea   North Island

                                                                    NEW
                                                                    ZEALAND
                                          South Island

dac

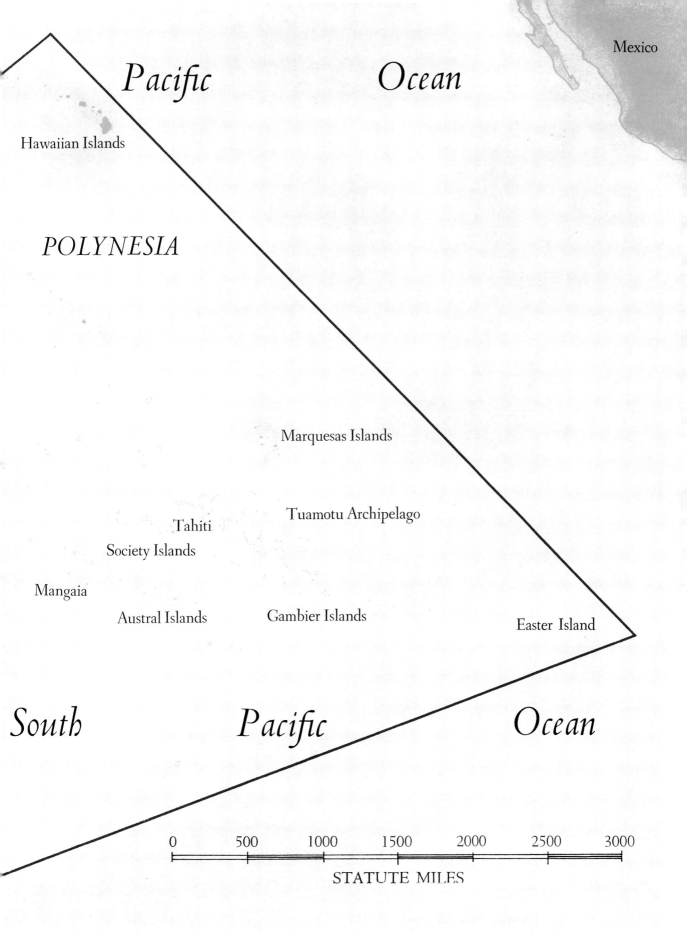

Pacific   Ocean

                                                        Mexico

Hawaiian Islands

POLYNESIA

                        Marquesas Islands

                            Tuamotu Archipelago

            Tahiti
        Society Islands

Mangaia

        Austral Islands   Gambier Islands

                                            Easter Island

South   Pacific   Ocean

        0   500   1000   1500   2000   2500   3000

                        STATUTE MILES

SLIT GONG. Ambrym Island, New Hebrides. 33″ x 4½″;
de Young Art Trust; #71.7.3.

FIGURE — PART OF A HOUSE POST. Tami Island,
Huon Gulf Region, New Guinea. 31½″ x 11″; Gift of Mr.
Leroy Buchignani; #46.18.

Melanesia

The artists of Melanesia were perhaps the most prolific in all the Pacific. Their sculpture and painting, architecture and other arts are dramatic and spectacular, often brilliantly colorful or constructed of strange and unusual materials, and fantastic, grotesque and transcendent in their imagery.

Wide diversity in form and style is characteristic of Melanesian art as a whole. Regional styles appear to have developed in relative isolation brought about by many factors, among them extreme differences in language and, especially, constant antagonism, warfare and head-hunting among local communities.

This wide formal and stylistic diversity belies certain basic similarities of meaning and function underlying much of Melanesian art. Many works were created to honor the souls of the ancestors and to serve as a point of contact between the living and the dead. Ancestor spirits, believed to watch over and to protect the living, were often honored in ceremonies held in conjunction with the initiation of youths into adulthood. The youths, through the initiation ritual, were symbolically reborn as adults, capable of taking their ultimate place as ancestral beings. This theme is reflected over and over in Melanesian art and myth.

The ancestors were not thought of as distant, aloof supernaturals but were often identified with deceased individuals remembered by the living members of the community. A memorial or commemorative mask or figure, for example, might bear the name of a particular person. The deceased's importance as an ancestor spirit sometimes mirrored his status in life. A courageous warrior, an industrious or lucky individual who had accumulated a degree of wealth or respect, all were more likely to be regarded after death as more powerful and important supernaturals than someone who had achieved little honor and prestige in life.

Supernaturals other than ancestors were thought to dwell in the sky or sea, in reefs or rocks, and had the power to affect the lives and fortunes of men. The boundary between ancestral spirits and those supernaturals of a non-ancestral, mythical character was not always clear cut, but the latter appear to have been only rarely depicted in art. Even the sea spirits represented in certain of the figures from the Solomons and masks from New Caledonia, for example, had strong relationships with ancestor worship. On the other hand, representations of totemic figures—such as mythical animals, symbolically linked to or regarded as progenitors of a lineage—took a prominent place in Melanesian iconography.

The concept of an all pervading, intangible, metaphysical energy or power, termed *mana* was the basis of much of Oceanic religion and ritual. Although not developed to such complexity as in Polynesia, it was found throughout Melanesia and in many ways had an effect on the visual forms of art. It was believed that man might control the power through magic and ritual but it could also be extremely dangerous to him. Inanimate as well as animate things could contain this force and, in Melanesian belief, it was a primary quality of the important ancestors. It was also contained in the bones of the dead, those of relatives as well as those of enemy victims of sacrifice or headhunting expeditions. The human skull was especially potent and was of considerable iconographic importance in many Melanesian art styles.

The artist in Melanesian society was not subject to a long period of apprenticeship as was customary, for example, in Polynesia. He usually had little formal training other than observing the older, skilled craftsmen in his village. The position of artist and craftsman was not typically hereditary. Usually anyone could aspire to be an artist, although it was the most gifted sculptor or painter in the community who was given the important commissions. A man's reputation as a fine artist afforded him respect and perhaps increased prosperity, but he could not support himself solely on the proceeds of his artistic endeavors.

The rituals which would be carried on during the creation of a work of art were primarily concerned with the ultimate success of the ceremony or event for which the object was being made rather than to insure the perfection of the object itself. In some instances, in fact, the work of art might even be discarded after use, having served its ritual purposes and being considered, perhaps, as too sacred and dangerous an item to be associated with day-to-day village life.

Ceremony and ritual in Melanesia focused upon the creation of a dramatic stage for the presentation of the initiates and for the symbolic appearance of the ancestors. Melanesian art was often made in secret, then brought out with colorful display and pageantry. Melanesian forms sought to impress, to dramatically create awe and fear in the viewer's eyes, and, in their bright

SHIELD. New Britain (collected before 1900). 51″ x 14″;
Gift of Mrs. Edwin Diamond, 1915; #41467.

LABUI MALANGGAN FIGURE. New Ireland (collected
before 1900). 57½″ x 7¼″; Gift of Mrs. Edwin Diamond,
1915; #41448.

LIME SPATULA. Trobriand Islands, New Guinea. 12⅛″
x 3¼″; Gift of the Henry Crocker Estate, 1961; #C173I.

FOOD POUNDER. Wamira District, Massim area, New
Guinea. 25″ x 5″; Gift of the Henry Crocker Estate, 1961;
#53-42-142.

color and fantastic shapes, recreate concepts of the universe of the imagined and the supernatural.

New Guinea   Religion and ceremony were not the only purposes for which art was created in Melanesia. There were many levels of meaning within each object and the context in which each functioned. Masks and ornaments permitted their wearers to associate with and transform themselves into the apparition of the supernatural. In addition, the human individuals underneath the disguise gained social prestige from this association and transformation. The sponsors of a particular event—the individual, clan or village providing the art objects, festive food and other necessities and payments for a ceremonial observance—gained not only the favor of the supernatural and high regard in the eyes of their fellow celebrants, but the event often had its return in economic and political advantages for those concerned. This multi-faceted aspect of artistic production becomes clearly apparent in the art of New Guinea.

New Guinea is one of the largest islands of the world and within its bounds there existed a number of art style provinces or geographical regions with a specific and distinctive style. To a significant degree, production of the plastic arts seems to have been limited to areas along the coast and the middle and lower courses of major rivers and their tributaries. The peoples of the interior mountainous areas, regions which have only recently been explored by outsiders, do not appear to have had important traditions of sculpture and painting.

Northwestern New Guinea   One of the most interesting but poorly known of these art style provinces is that of the Geelvink Bay and adjacent areas of West Irian. The art from this region is sometimes said to belong to the *korwar* style because of a distinctive type of small ancestor carving known as *korwar* which appears to have been a dominant but by no means the only art form produced in this region. Early observers wrote of sculptured architectural decorations, carved canoe prows and shields, but today these other art forms are exceedingly rare.

In comparison with New Guinea's other, more monumental art styles, *korwar* figures are relatively small in scale and at first glance appear to have an unusual homogeneity of form. These carvings have a rounded base upon which stands or sits a human figure with rudimentary body and much en-

KORWAR FIGURE. Geelvink Bay, West Irian. 10″ x 5⅜″; Gift of the Henry Crocker Estate; #59.12.3.

larged head. The figure usually holds a shield or openwork scroll-like element in front of the body. The wood is dark and polished and seldom shows any trace of color other than that of glass trade beads set in the eyes.

In each *korwar* is believed to dwell the spirit of a particular deceased individual. The figure serves primarily as a means of communication between the spirit of the dead and its living descendants. It is made during the time of mourning and the carver also possessed the magic to entice the soul of the deceased into the sculpture. *Korwar* figures were considered to be protectors of the household and would even be taken on dangerous journeys to keep the family from harm. The sculpture also acted as a divinitory device or oracle when the ancestral spirit dwelling within would be asked for advice. Offerings of tobacco or small bits of cloth were made while the supplicant waited to feel some sign, perhaps a trembling sensation in his limbs or body, which would answer his question. When the *korwar* figure was felt to have ceased its effectiveness or protection it was discarded.

MAPRIK DISTRICT, NEW GUINEA   In many regions of New Guinea a great deal of artistic effort was devoted to building the men's ceremonial house or cult house. This edifice which was usually decorated with painting and sculpture was also the storehouse for ceremonial art and served to shelter the artist while he worked. The most complex of these ceremonial houses were to be found among the Abelam tribesmen who live in the Maprik district north of the Sepik River, an area of precipitious mountains and dense tropical forest.

The impressive ceremonial structures of the Abelam were built facing a wide plaza and stood up to 60 or 80 feet in height. The upper section of the roughly triangular facade was completely decorated with rows of enormous heads brightly painted on sheets of bark. Carved figures and panels were attached below. The carvings were also covered with the red, yellow, black and white pigments utilized for the bark paintings and added to the vividly colorful aspect of the house. Sculptures of a more sacred nature representing both male and female ancestors were stood up along the walls inside the ceremonial house. Despite the presence of female ancestor images inside the structure, however, the interior was forbidden to women except upon the occasion of the inauguration of the house.

The cult house, its carvings and the rituals and activities which took place within it were closely linked with the aspirations of the male members of the Abelam villages for prestige and status. As they often do elsewhere, such aspirations took on a curious form. Among the Abelam, prestige and authority was conferred upon those men who were able to grow the largest yams. The men in the community participated in the yam cult which consisted of a complex series of rites and activities to promote the growth of a species of yam *Dioscorea alata* which could reach an extraordinary length of up to 12 feet. Cult magic was also designed to make the yams of rival growers magically diminish in size or, preferably, even rot in the ground.

The ancestors who were represented by the sculptured figures inside the ceremonial house were believed to aid in the growth of the yams and they were honored when the harvest was displayed on the dance plaza fronting the ceremonial house. For this display, the yams were tied to poles and decorated with woven and painted basketry masks, cassowary feathers, flowers and orna-

ANCESTOR FIGURE
FROM *TAMBERAN*
HOUSE. Abelam, Maprik
area, New Guinea. 46″ x 9½″;
Gift of Mr. Victor Bergeron;
#58.27.5.

ments of shell. The yams were believed to embody certain aspects of the ancestral spirits and the largest of the yams were named after important ancestors and paraded through the village. Later, they were exchanged with rival yam growers who, it was hoped, would feel shame if their own yams were not as large.

Abelam art differs from the traditional styles of the nearby Sepik River area in its emphasis upon color rather than upon sculptural shape and volume. Abelam figures are simply rendered as a series of juxtaposed ovals and crescent forms while details of body and facial features, ornament and other patterning devices were not carved into the wood but painted over the surface in the vivid colors characteristic of this style.

SUSPENSION HOOK. Huon Gulf, New Guinea (collected before 1900). 15½″ x 4½″; California Midwinter International Exposition, 1895; #2177.

CANOE SPLASH BOARD. Trobriand Islands, New Guinea (collected before 1900). 24″ x 15½″; California Midwinter International Exposition, 1895; #2146C.

MASSIM DISTRICT, NEW GUINEA   The art of the Massim district differs from other New Guinea styles in its preference for designs of an almost abstract nature and in its focus on the decoration of primarily utilitarian objects. There was an emphasis on decorative ornamentation consisting of elaborate spirals, scrolls and delicate pierced openwork rendered by incorporating stylized figures of long-beaked birds, crocodiles and humans into the geometric designs. Three dimensional figure sculpture other than that used in these ornamental compositions was relatively rare. Colors—specifically red, white and black—were applied only to certain kinds of objects such as war shields, dance wands and canoe prows, apparently endowing these kinds of objects with greater magic or sacredness than those unpainted. On other types of carving, contrast was achieved by the juxtaposition of dark polished wood and white lime rubbed into the finely incised lines or contours on the surface of the object.

Although the Massim style province encompasses the southeastern tip of mainland New Guinea and several off-shore island groups, the best known examples of this style come from the Trobriand Islands. Here, a number of art forms were made in connection with a highly organized system of cere-

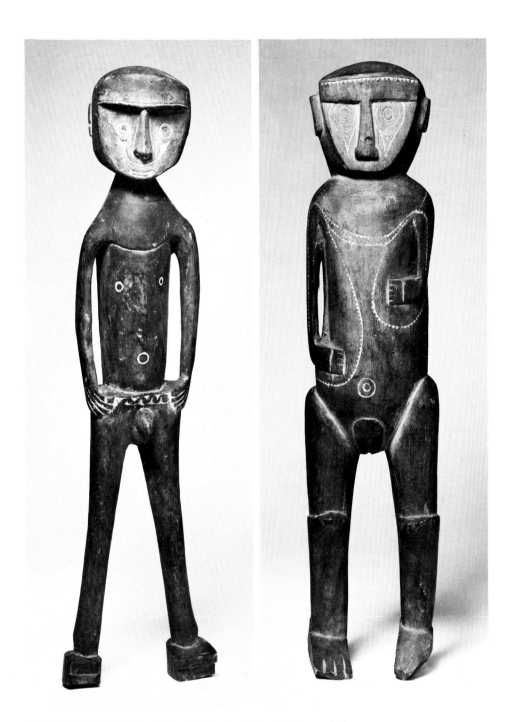

MALE FIGURE. Trobriand Islands, New Guinea (collected before 1900). 20½″ x 3″; California Midwinter International Exposition, 1895; #2157B.

FEMALE FIGURE. Trobriand Islands, New Guinea (collected before 1900). 20½″ x 4½″; California Midwinter International Exposition, 1895; #2157A.

monial exchange known as the *kula*. The participants in these transactions exchanged rare items—shell discs, arm bands and polished stone blades—with specific trading partners in far-off villages, sometimes requiring open sea voyages of considerable distance.

The type of sailing craft used by the Trobriand traders was a single outrigger dugout canoe. These were handsome vessels and were built or repaired just prior to the time of the *kula* exchange. Appropriate magic accompanied all such activities to insure that the canoe be safe and swift and also that the exchange be advantageous for the owner of the canoe and its crew. Particularly elaborate magic and ritual was carried out when the decorated splash boards were affixed to a new vessel.

The same intricate curvilinear patterns and open work carved into the canoe splash boards occur on delicately sculptured dance wands. The dances in which participants carried these wands were part of an elaborate month-long feast which was held at the time of the yam harvest. At this occasion, as among many other peoples elsewhere in New Guinea, thanksgiving was made to the ancestors for successful crops and benefits received by the community during the year.

MORTAR AND PESTLE. Trobriand Islands, New Guinea. 5″ x 1″; Gift of the Henry Crocker Estate, 1916; #C175C.

DANCE WAND OR ORNAMENT. Trobriand Islands,
New Guinea (collected before 1900). 28½″ x 10¾″; California Midwinter International Exposition, 1895; #2144.

OUTRIGGER CANOE MODEL. Trobriand Islands, New
Guinea. 32½″ x 48″; Gift of Mr. T. Crocker, date unknown;
#X71.35.

New Ireland   In the northern districts of New Ireland much of the regional artistic production was destined for memorial ceremonies known as *malanggan* and this style is sometimes called the *malanggan* style. The artists of New Ireland, emphasizing exaggerated, inventive shapes, bright color patterning and consistent use of delicate openwork created a wide variety of unusual forms. Such innovation seems to have taken place in response to the particular function of *malanggan* art and, even more specifically, to the highly unusual manner in which the artist received his vision of the object he was to create.

The presentation of the *malanggan* festival required many works of art. It was an occasion of major importance, held to honor and mourn the dead, as well as to initiate and circumcise the young boys in the community. Preparation for the feast took almost a year, perhaps longer, to complete. Months before the main event, magicians made rain and garden magic to insure ample crops for the celebration. The *malanggan* sculptures also had to be commissioned and carried out months in advance. Each clan owned the design for a particular sculpture, which consisted of various life forms and symbolic shapes juxtaposed to create large anthropomorphic or zoomorphic figures, friezes or entire mythical scenes. Each sculpture was a composite of many different elements such as human figures, fish, birds, snakes as well as symbolic representations of celestial bodies. Certain motifs were regarded as symbols of the deceased ancestors, some were merely decorative while others, the moon and sun, for example, were involved with the more abstract mythology of New Ireland society.

Since the majority of sculptures created for the *malanggan* ceremony were destroyed after the completion of the ritual, the individual designs had to be retained in the memory of the clan headman. When new *malanggan* rites were to be held or when a neighboring clan purchased the rights to use the design, a skilled carver was commissioned to recreate the particular sculpture. A special house was constructed for the artist and, as he worked, the clan headman carefully directed how the carving should be shaped and painted. The fact that these design forms were transferred from owner to artist conceptually rather than visually appears to have allowed for considerable formal innovation, all, however, within the limits of the society's aesthetic code.

Certain rites were undertaken at specific steps in the carving process, at the moment of placing the sea snail opercula for the eyes of the figure, for example, or when the sculpture was painted with its coat of white base paint.

At each of these steps the artist followed a prescribed sequence in his work process.

At the climax of the *malanggan* ceremony when the young circumcised initiates returned from a period of seclusion, the sculptures were displayed in a gallery-like enclosure and the community assembled to honor and mourn its deceased ancestors. When the feast was completed the different carvings were carried out to the bush and left to rot. Having served their purpose, they were believed to be deeply connected to the spirit world and were therefore dangerous to the living when the community again resumed its ordinary day-to-day existence.

The *tatanua* or funerary masks were not destroyed after the *malanggan* festival, unlike most of the other art objects created for this ceremonial display. These masks were worn by dancers who participated in the *malanggan* rites and represented the ancestral spirits. Villagers clearly associated the different *tatanua* masks with specific deceased relatives and believed the mask wearers to be the reincarnation or reappearance of the spirit of that individual.

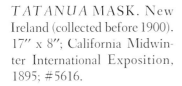

TATANUA MASK. New Ireland (collected before 1900). 17″ x 8″; California Midwinter International Exposition, 1895; #5616.

MALANGGAN CARVING. New Ireland (collected before 1900).
40¼″ x 14″; California Midwinter International Exposition, 1895;
#5515.

JANUS HAT MASK *(temes mbalmbal)*. Malekula, New Hebrides.
35½″ x 9″; de Young Art Trust; #71.7.1.

New Hebrides   A characteristic element in the art style of the New Hebrides is the imaginative and ingenious use of strange and unusual materials for the construction of a work of art. In addition to wood and stone, tree fern, vegetable composte, mud, feathers, leaves, pigs tusks, even the thick web of a large species of spider imparted diverse tactile, color and form impressions. This aided the task of the New Hebrides artist to create a variety of different categories of art works, serving as kinds of insignia to define an individual's rank within several graded societies.

Certain of these societies appear to have been on the order of secular associations, others were sacred. Both types, however, were closely related with almost parallel series of ranks or grades and initiation procedures. A man usually belonged to both, entering the lowest grades as a boy. He could rise from rank to rank through payments to members of each aspired grade and thus achieved increasing political authority and ritual status.

The celebration of a man's entrance to a higher rank and the prerogatives of membership were expressed in specific art forms. In the primarily secular societies, large human figures of tree fern were set up in the dance plaza in front of the men's ceremonial house as part of the ceremony to mark an individual's entrance into one of the lower grades while stone and wood figures were permitted to those entering higher ranks.

In Malekula, hat masks or headdresses called *temes mbalmbal* served this same function in the essentially sacred graded societies. Hat masks belonging to each successive grade were of different shape and form. *Temes* is the word for soul or ghost and these elaborate constructions were regarded as the temporary abode of the ancestral spirits. The masks belonging to lower grades were far simpler than those belonging to the higher grades. A child entering a lower level, for example, might wear a conical hat mask decorated with feathers but with no sculptured features. Hat masks with two, three or four faces were of increasingly higher rank, while among initiates to the highest grades, grotesque and brightly painted full figures were worn as constructions on top of the head.

The candidate to a higher rank was required to buy his way up, and large payments for admission were made to those men who were already members of that grade. Payments were in the form of pigs which were the measure of a man's wealth. The New Hebridians' penchant for rank was even extended to these animals which were graded according to age and growth of tusk. Only boars were considered to be valuable for ceremonial exchange. When young, the pig's upper canines were knocked out, permitting the lower tusks to grow, sometimes to a full circle. The most highly valued animals were those whose tusks pierced through the jaw to grow out again. Such pigs were considered fitting payment for admission to the highest ranks.

The rites of the *nevinbur*, another sacred society, were elaborate and, at certain times, took on the character of a dramatic performance. For this a great number of sculptures were required including life-size figures of a mythical hero named Manship and his two wives, smaller images of their numerous offspring, and various other, puppet-like figures. The brightly painted representations of the hero and his wives were set up in front of the men's ceremonial house and a fence was constructed behind them as a back drop. Tubes of bamboo were buried in the ground beneath the figures, extending behind the fence. The tubes were used to carry the voices of the spirits which were projected from behind the fence by members of the *nevinbur* society. Small grotesquely modelled heads or puppet-like figures were affixed to the end of long sticks. They bobbed up and down behind the fence and seemed to be dancing to the audience of women and the uninitiated. At one time during the *nevinbur* rites several of the smaller spirit figures were deliberately destroyed and a large series of new ones were then made, an act which appears closely involved with the concept, widespread in Melanesia, that death or symbolic destruction must precede the process of creation.

PUPPET. Malekula, New Hebrides. 31″ x 7″; de Young Art Trust; 71.7.2.

ANCESTOR FIGURE. Maori, New Zealand. 19¼″ x 3¾″;
de Young Art Trust; #71.19.1.

CANOE PROW (*tauihu*). Maori, New Zealand (collected
before 1900). 22¼″ x 46¼″; California Midwinter International Exposition, 1895; #5524.

Polynesia

Polynesia presents many distinct contrasts to Melanesia. This region, which encompasses the vast eastern area of the south Pacific, is sparsely dotted with tiny islands and island archipelagos—some such as New Zealand and Hawaii—as much as 4500 miles distant one from the other. No matter how remote or isolated, however, the peoples of Polynesia were unusually homogeneous in culture, in language and even in their physical appearance.

The Polynesians, as did the Melanesians long before them, seem to have come originally from southeast Asia. Exactly when the first eastward migrations began is still unknown but archaeological evidence indicates that voyagers had reached western Polynesia early in the first millenium B.C. and Easter Island shortly after the beginning of the Christian era. There is no evidence of any migration westward from South America. Peruvian artifacts found on Easter Island and sometimes cited as proof of the New World origin of the Polynesians all date after the Spanish conquest of the Inca Empire, centuries after the establishment of all Polynesian societies. On the other hand, the Polynesians were master seafarers and could conceivably have reached the Pacific coasts of the New World. Nonetheless, no shred of evidence has been found to indicate any form of prehistoric contact between the two regions.

Polynesian religion and myth, the philosophical concepts upon which man based his interaction with the gods and with other men, and the power and status accorded to different groups in the society were interlinked with the specific forms of art. Religious belief centered about a highly complex pantheon of deities, of which the most important were the god of the sea, the sky god and the god of vegetation and war. Each locality had its district gods, the patron deities of crafts and occupation, and deified chiefs, priests and ancestors. Sculptural representations of the great gods exist but they are exceedingly rare and may be highly abstract in form, even simplified to basketry cones or lengths of wood wrapped in *tapa* cloth. The lesser deities and ancestral beings were usually more conventionally sculptured as anthropomorphic forms.

Concern with status, with the formal observations of respect and privilege, and with *mana,* the concept of intangible, supernatural, impersonal power was paramount. The Polynesians believed that *mana* was present in all persons and things to a greater or lesser degree depending on the prestige, worth or effectiveness of the person or object. Persons of the highest social rank were thought to possess the greatest amount of this power. Among many groups, the elite traced its ancestry directly from the gods and through this line of descent came great and potent *mana.* It could be gained especially through elaborate ritual. While undertaking the task of canoe building, figure carving, even painful and elaborate tattooing operations, the artist or craftsman carried out specific rites to insure the success of his work and to instill it with this power. On the other hand, *mana* could be lost through defilement—contact or involvement with something impure or having lesser *mana.* Thus, the system of *tapu* or prohibition against such contact was developed and served not only religious ends but as an efficient means of social control as well.

In Polynesia, the artist was called *tohunga* or some slight variation, a title implying sacredness. Priests were also *tohunga,* and the artist-craftsman was considered the priest of the god of his particular craft. Unlike the relatively casual training of the aspiring artist in Melanesia, the Polynesian youth underwent a long period of apprenticeship. During this time he not only learned mastery of style and techniques but all the important rituals and prayers to accompany the act of artistic creativity.

In Polynesia, as elsewhere, an important prerogative of status was wealth, and wealth was, in part, measured by possession of works of art. A beautifully made house, war canoes, carved weapons and utensils, ornaments and feather garments, even the elegance of body tattooing were frequently the marks of chiefly or kingly power. It is primarily these forms which comprise the major portion of Polynesian art.

Unlike Melanesian art with its extravagant use of color, the Polynesian artist sought to bring out the beauty and essence of the material with which he was working and seldom used paint to cover sculptural forms. In comparison with the art of Melanesia, Polynesian styles appear more static and rigid. Similar forms occur over and over and only as a rare exception did the artist depart from the established pattern and attempt a degree of major formal or stylistic innovation. The beauty of Polynesian art is just in the perfection and harmonious repetition or, more frequently, the exceedingly subtle variation

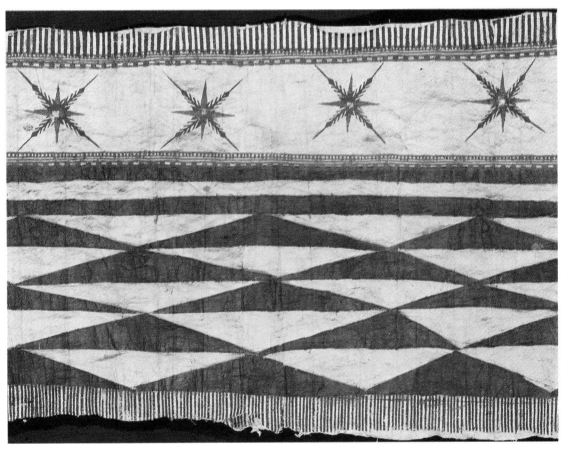

TAPA CLOTH. Samoa. 531″ x 21½″; Gift of Mrs. Elsa
Weber; #62.30.2.

BOWLS (*umeke*). Hawaiian Islands. 8½″ x 10¾″; 7″ x 5¾″;
Gift of Mary Beardsley; #47.23.1 & 5.

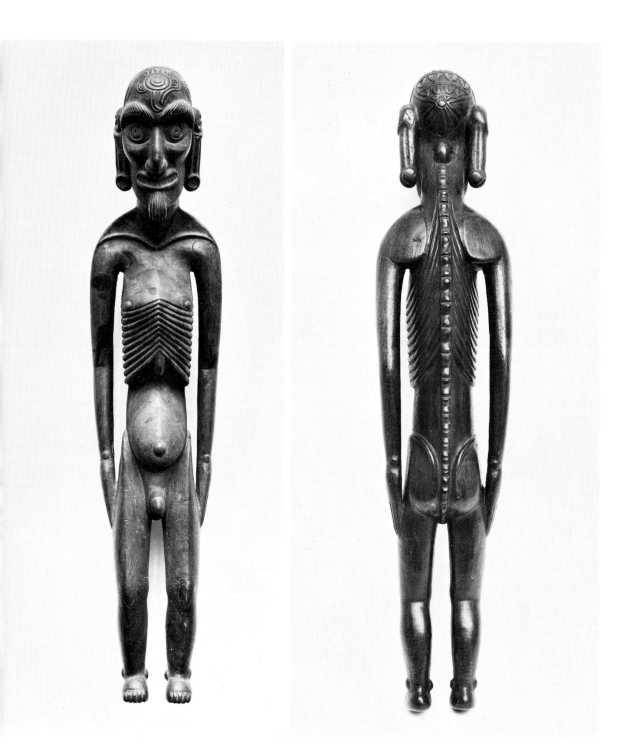

MALE ANCESTOR FIGURE (front and back views).
Easter Island. 17½″ x 4″; Gift of Mr. William R. Hearst,
1931; #53743.

of established forms. Even utensils, weapons and other items carved without surface embellishment were works of art simply in the excellence of their shape and execution.

EASTER ISLAND   Tiny Easter Island lies at the remote eastern edge of Polynesia. It is barren and windswept, unlike the lush tropical islands of central Polynesia. Easter Island is best known for its megalithic art, spectacular stone images carved as schematic human figures. There are many hundreds of these sculptures, some are small examples several feet high, others are enormous figures weighing over 100 tons. A number were found set up on the slopes of Rano Raraku, the mountain quarry on the eastern side of the island, but others were originally erected on stone platforms built along the island's coastline. These platforms were shrines or temples belonging to the different, rival lineages of Easter Island. The sculptures which represented the power and prestige of the lineages seem to have been memorials or portraits of the most important chiefs within each group.

Less spectacular but more aesthetically powerful are smaller sculptures carved in wood. Wood was scarce on Easter Island and whatever was available was considered precious, especially the branches of the *toro miro* bush, which although stunted and twisted in shape, could be polished to a dark lustrous finish. These wood figures are characteristically small, finely carved and elegantly finished. They take the shape of long beaked birds with twisted human-like bodies, lizards and emaciated human figures which are believed to represent the honored ancestors associated with fertility and the harvest.

From archaeologists' accounts of the ancient temple ruins on Easter Island, early ritual practices involved some form of solar worship, possibly directed toward the god Tane. After a period of tribal warfare and upheaval in the 17th century, the warrior class took political control from the more ancient ruling lineages. The warriors adopted as their special god the deity Makemake, believed to bring the sea birds each year to nest on the island. The eggs of the sea birds were a valuable source of food. During the annual festival of the cult of the bird man, the important island chiefs competed to win the title of Bird Man, regarded as the incarnation of Makemake. The winner of the competition was then sanctified for the following year. Ancestor figures seem to have been in some way associated with the power of the bird deity, and on many of these emaciated figures the bald cranium is carved with the bird design in low relief.

FOOD BOWL. Marquesas Islands. 9⅜″ diameter; Gift of Mary Beardsley; #47.23.11.

THE MARQUESAS ISLANDS   The 19th century novels of Herman Melville, written about his adventures in the Marquesas, brought these islands to the attention of the outside world. They drew an artist's imaginative picture of the South Seas but in actuality, the Marquesas are not the paradise described. They are rugged volcanic islands with precipitious mountains, deep valleys, areas of lush vegetation alternating with areas of more barren terrain. From time to time, long and severe periods of drought brought famine and distress to the island populations. In the past, there was incessant competition for the more fertile valleys and Marquesan oral tradition relates a long history of bitter warfare among neighboring tribes. Archaeological evidence indicates that the earliest migrants to Hawaii and Easter Island may have come from the Marquesas, perhaps forced by famine or war in their homeland to immigrate to new, uncharted islands.

In the traditional art of the Marquesas, the human figure was an important element but it was always highly conventionalized and variation in its form and features was always subtle. Large and small images in stone, bone, ivory and wood, tiny decorative figures carved on jewelry and ornaments, and

WARRIOR'S CLUB. Marquesas Islands. 45″ x 7″; Gift of the Henry Crocker Estate; #61.1.1.

relief designs covering the surfaces of utensils and weapons—all depicted the characteristic, conventionalized figure with large eyes, square chin and squat pose which was known by the term *tiki*. The word *tiki* or its variations means a representation of a human or human-like figure in Polynesian dialects. These could also take the shape of small repeated patterns representing parts of figures such as a hand or heavy lidded circular eye combined to create an almost abstract pattern over the surface of the sculpture.

MANGAIA   The god Tane was considered by many of the island peoples to be the creator god, the source of light, fecundity and knowledge, and the representation of the male principle. In ancient times, according to legend, Tane was the most important of the gods. But during later struggles for power between ambitious warrior groups and the traditional ruling aristocracy, the importance of Tane waned and the prestige of the war god increased.

Tane remained, however, as the god of artistic creativity, the patron of crafts-men—the carpenter, wood sculptors, canoe makers and house builders.

Decorated adzes were associated with the creator deity in Mangaia, one of several large islands in the Cook archipelago in central Polynesia. Here, Tane was also called "Tane, Piler-up of Wood" or "Tane, Shearer of Thatch" and was embodied and venerated in the form of the sacred stone adzes used in making ceremonial objects. Magaian adzes were fitted with large handles to serve as mounts or pedestals which were characteristically incised with delicate geometric patterns forming a repeated double K motif. This motif is thought to represent a stylized human figure. Most of these decorated adzes were not actually used as tools. The largest and most spectacular examples seem to have been carved in post-missionary times but may reflect the more ancient sacred forms in shape and decoration.

NEW ZEALAND   The Maori of New Zealand were among the most prolific artists in Polynesia. Their characteristic style with its elaborate curvilinear surface ornamentation is unique and, except for the women's art of weaving, was consistent throughout from wood carving to ornate patterns of facial and body tattooing.

Much of Maori art was devoted to architectural decoration. A number of different types of houses were to be found in Maori villages, each built for a different function and each varying as to the elegance of its decoration, strength and durability. There were rude structures for cooking and more substantial houses for sleeping and to shelter the canoes. But the most impor-tant and elegantly decorated structures were the large meeting or superior houses and the *pataka* or elevated storehouses. In Maori myth, the art of building and decorating these important structures was divine knowledge given to man by the gods, and each building had an individual name, given in memory of an ancestor or derived from some important event. Such houses were not to be found in every village but only in the rich and more powerful settlements and their presence lent prestige to all members of the community.

Both the elevated storehouse and the superior house were gabled build-ings with a deep front porch. The storehouse, though elevated on poles, was essentially a small version of the superior house but often even more highly decorated. On each type of building the barge boards, gable ornament, sup-port posts and threshold boards were usually carved. The interior walls of the superior house consisted of sections of colorfully patterned lashing alternating

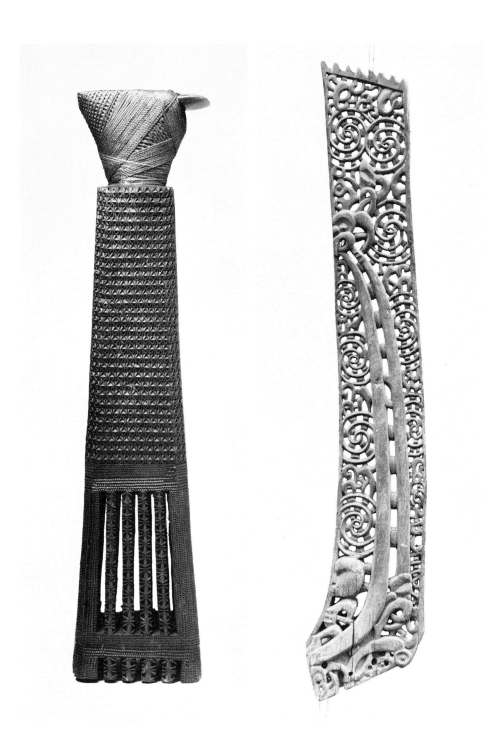

CEREMONIAL ADZE. Mangaia Island, Cook Islands
Group (collected before 1900). 22″ x 4¼″; California Midwinter International Exposition, 1895; #2224.

CANOE STERN ORNAMENT. Maori, New Zealand
(collected before 1900). 65″ x 12½″; California Midwinter
International Exposition, 1895; #5525.

GABLE FIGURE *(teko teko)*. Maori, New Zealand. 30⅜″ x 4⅜″;
de Young Art Trust; #71.19.4.

with large wood panels. The wood panels, their bases set into the ground and upper sections shaped to support the rafters, were sculptured in relief with designs representing ancestral or mythical figures.

Some groups, constantly at war and continually apprehensive against attack, constructed major fortifications around their settlements. These fortified villages were the famous Maori *pa,* marvelled at by early European voyagers in New Zealand. The settlement site was initially chosen for its strategic location usually on a high, easily defensible hill or escarpment. In the village area one or more great trenches would be dug and the excavated earth piled up to form high ramparts. On the ramparts and beyond the trenches, tall stockades of strong timbers would be erected.

NEPHRITE PENDANT (*hei tiki*). Maori, New Zealand. 4½″ x 2⅞″; Gift of M. H. de Young, 1915; #41524.

Maori preoccupation with battle, revenge and the status accrued to the victor is reflected in the magnificence of their war canoes, and even more clearly, in the elegance of their fighting weapons. The fierceness and courage of the Maori warrior is legendary. Young men of high rank were trained for war and were dedicated to the war god from infancy. Warriors fought for booty and spoils, for captives and to gain revenge for insults or quarrels with their rivals. Among the Maori, war was thought of as the "great game."

Rather than projectile weapons, various types of thrusting spears, striking clubs and daggers were preferred, for it was thought that the most glorious fighting was to engage the enemy in hand-to-hand combat. These finely wrought and carefully decorated weapons were emblems of status.

WHALEBONE CLUB (*patu daraoa*). Maori, New Zealand.
14¼″ x 3¾″; Gift of M. H. de Young, 1915; #41527.

ANCESTOR FIGURE. Maori, New Zealand (collected before 1900). 25⅜″ x 6″; California Midwinter International Exposition, 1895; #5523.

ARCHITECTURAL PANEL (*pou pou*). Maori, New Zealand. 89½″ x 17″; de Young Art Trust; #71.19.3.

ANCESTOR FIGURE OF KOTUWHAKA IRIORA. Maori, New Zealand (collected before 1900). 55½″ x 7½″; California Midwinter International Exposition, 1895; #5522.

LINTEL CARVING *(pare)*. Maori, New Zealand. 21″ x 59½″; de Young Art Trust; #71.19.2.

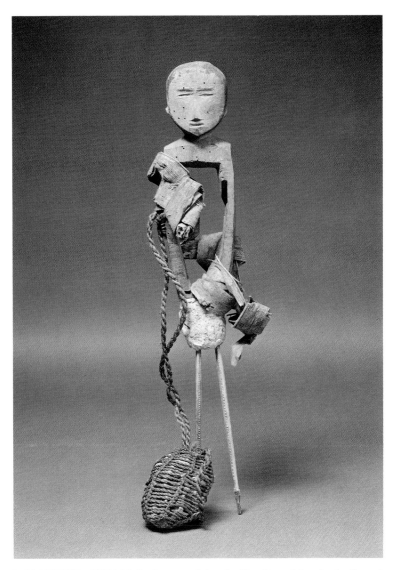

WEATHER CHARM. Onoum Island, Caroline Islands (collected before 1900). 16″ x 3″; gift of Park Commission, 1905; #26168.

Micronesia

In many of the Micronesian islands, crafts rather than sculpture or painting were developed to a high degree. There is ample evidence of this in the fine jewelry and ornaments, matting, basketry, decorated fabrics, finely made weapons and tools from this region. It is not known whether sculpture and painting flourished abundantly in earlier times and disappeared prior to contact with the west or whether such means of artistic expression were ever utilized with any frequency in Micronesia.

Among the rare examples of Micronesian sculpture are unusual figures fitted with sting ray spines at their base. These were weather charms placed on the bow of a canoe as a protective device. In case of a threatening storm, a priest or magician would raise the charm against the supernatural forces to prevent danger and to calm the sea.

TATOO COMBS. Caroline Islands. 1½″ x 4¾″; Gift of Park Commission, 1905; #26177A.

NORTH AMERICA

Arctic
Ocean

Eskimo

Aleut

Eskimo

Eskimo

Eskimo

NORTHWEST

COAST

INDIANS

Tlingit

Eskimo

Eskimo

Hudson Bay

Tsimshian

Haida

Bella Coola

Kwakiutl

Nootka

Salish

Cree

PLAINS

INDIANS

Ojibwa

Nez Perce

Missouri

Crow

Yurok

GREAT

Pomo

BASIN

Miwok

Shoshoni

Costanoan

CALIFORNIA

Yokut

INDIANS

INDIANS

Cheyenne

Sioux

Sauk

Fox

Iroquois

Arapaho

River

Chumash

Navajo

EASTERN

Hopi

WOODLANDS

Zuñi

Acoma

Kiowa

Mississippi

SOUTHWEST

Apache

INDIANS

INDIANS

River

Creek

Pacific

Ocean

Atlantic

Ocean

NORTHERN

MEXICO

Gulf of Mexico

Caribbean Sea

200 100 0 200 400 600 800
STATUTE MILES

dac

Introduction

The forebears of the American Indian entered the New World in the remote past of the Pleistocene or Glacial Age, perhaps, say some scholars, as many as twenty to thirty thousand years ago. These are very early estimates for the arrival of Paleo-Indian, as the first inhabitants of the Americas are called, and are presently much in dispute. There is no doubt, however, that by at least 12,000 years ago, man was firmly established in both North and South America. Coming originally across northern Asia, the migrants ventured eastward during a period of advancing glacial ice when sea levels were lowered and a land bridge connected Siberia and Alaska. It is presumed that the newcomers were hunters and first entered the American continent (of course, unaware of their discovery) following herds of now extinct Pleistocene animals. We still know relatively little about the Paleo-Indian groups although increasingly more information about them and their way of life is being uncovered by New World archaeologists. We cannot as yet say that there were artists among them. However, the very fineness of their chipped stone implements and the occasional use of beautifully colored stone which seems to have been carried considerable distance from its source, could argue at least for the beginnings of aesthetic involvement.

Unlike the Indians of both Mesoamerica and Andean South America whose arts were either submerged beneath the influence of imported European styles or disappeared completely after the Conquest, the majority of North American peoples continued their artistic production, in some instances even more vigorously, after European contact. However, the impact of the foreigner's products, styles and culture always produced change, and each of the major North American art traditions are divided into prehistoric and historic periods. In some cases there is a very definite separation between the two periods in style and media as well as in form and function of the arts, in others there is a clear continuum from prehistoric times to the present.

One of the major changes to be seen in the historic period is the use of many imported products in art. The American Indian artist clearly enjoyed exploring the possibilities of new and varied raw materials. Perhaps this is

MASK. Eskimo, St. Michaels, Alaska. 10″ x 11¼″; Gift of Mrs. Edwin Diamond, 1915; #41478A.

ARGILLITE CARVING OF SHAMAN WITH TWO FIGURES.
Haida, Northwest Coast. 14″ x 10″; Lent Anonymously, 1911;
#4876L.

CHILKAT BLANKET. Tlingit, Northwest Coast. 64″ x
50″; de Young Trust Fund; #72.38.

one of the reasons why European products were so quickly incorporated into many Indian styles. Glass beads, trade cloth, silver, commercial paints and dyes, mirrors and the like were eagerly sought for the new color and textural dimensions which they could add to the work of art or craft. But this interest in the bright and novel was not something new for the Indian artist. On the contrary, it was many centuries old. In prehistoric times, rare and exotic products were often obtained by means of widespread trade networks. Obsidian, mica, sea shells from both Oceans, turquoise, copper, all were among the basic materials traded over long distances and at much effort.

It is difficult to generalize about American Indian art, for its primary characteristic is that of extraordinary diversity. Each regional and even tribal group maintained its unique style tradition within which could be found a multitude of localized variations and specializations. It is even more difficult to characterize the North American Indian artist. In some societies, the artist was a professional, paid for his services and fully trained by a master craftsman during a period of apprenticeship. In other groups, the artist was the shaman or curer, called upon by the spirits to make his visions clear to other mortals through his art. The shamans, in close touch with the supernatural through dreams or trances, were often creative and innovative individuals who could translate this vision experience into art or symbolize it in the iconography of their masks, charms, dance rattles and other magical paraphernalia.

Although the artists involved with the production of religious and ritual objects were usually men, most secular art was produced by the Indian women. Women were the potters in Pueblo society, the weavers among the Navaho, the basketmakers in California and the skin workers and embroiderers of quills and beads among the Plains tribes.

North American Indian art is therefore as diverse as the artists, the materials and the traditions allow. It is precisely this diversity and independence of tradition which makes this art unique and important.

THE DACOTA WOMAN. Print from original painting by Carl
Bodmer, 1832–33. Collection of the Haffenreffer Museum of Anthropology, Brown University.

Plains

"The Indians of the Plains are a fine and noble race. They are tall and graceful in their movements and wear pictured robes of the buffalo hide with pleasing effect," wrote George Catlin, the painter who documented Indian life in the mid-19th century. "They are good hunters," he observed, "and living in a country abounding with buffaloes, are well supplied with the necessities of life."*

The Great Plains, the heartland of the North American continent, spread monotonously and almost unbroken from Texas to northern Canada and from the Rockies almost to the Mississippi River. Before white settlers came to farm this land, the eastern regions or prairies were characterized by a tall grass savannah while a short grass vegetation was typical of the more arid western Plains. This ecological shift corresponded to a division of cultural pattern. Until the pressure of an expanding white population on the Atlantic seaboard forced them westward, the eastern prairie peoples lived in semi-permanent villages and were agriculturalists, depending secondarily upon hunting for their livelihood. In the high Plains of the west, however, population was sparser but the way of life of its early inhabitants more closely resembled our concept of the classic nomadic Plains Indian. They lived by hunting the buffalo which once existed in such vast numbers that early observers described the herds as appearing as "an endless sea" across the grassy terrain. The buffalo or, more accurately, the bison was the mainstay of life on the high Plains. It not only provided the hunter with his basic source of food but served as raw material for the manufacture of life's other necessities. Its skin was used for many articles of clothing, served as bedding and as a cover for the tipi or portable tent which sheltered the Indian family. Rawhide was made into food containers, carrying cases and war shields. Buffalo bone, horn and sinew were fashioned into weapons, rope, tools and utensils. Its fat, brains and other internal organs aided in tanning the hide and its woolly head was sometimes worn as a ceremonial headdress. It is not surprising then, that the bison figured prominently in the myth and ritual of the Plains Indian peoples and was a significant motif in their art.

From earliest times, the bison and other game had been taken with

---

* George Catlin, *Letters and Notes on the Manners, Customs, and Condition of the American Indians.*

spear, or bow and arrow. The hunter, disguised in animal skins, stalked stray-ing individuals on foot or caused a herd to stampede over a cliff or into a canyon where the kill was made. In the historic period, the arrival of the horse and fire arms made hunting easier, turned warfare and raiding into an exciting and prestigeous game, and in many other ways, had a profound effect upon Indian culture in this area. Despite Spanish efforts to prevent the In-dian from obtaining the horse, it had already fallen into the hands of Pueblo and Apache groups by the end of the 16th century and not much more than a hundred years later, it was to be found throughout most of central North America. The rifle, not being a self-reproducing commodity like the horse, traveled more slowly, reaching the Plains from the Northeast along the routes of the trappers and fur traders. Horses meant wealth and their acquisition became a primary motivation for warfare and raiding. An elaborate code of fighting was developed in Plains society which accorded rank and status to men of courage and leadership, qualities which an individual could only possess through the favorable intervention of the supernatural. These many social and economic factors molded and were reflected in the art of the Plains Indian peoples.

The most prominent aspects of Plains Indian art are those elaborate forms associated with honor and prestige and which were created for display. Art was an essential medium through which a family could show its wealth and a warrior could boast of his courage in both symbolic and depictive form. The artistic tradition which developed upon this basis emphasized decora-tion of oneself and one's costume, and the embellishment of the useful things closely associated with the individual such as his dwelling and its furnishings, the trappings of his horse, his weapons and war shield. Elegant costume was decorated with brightly colored beaded, quilled or painted patterns, fringes, metal tinkling cones and horse, or sometimes human, hair locks. Added to the effect were splendid headdresses of eagle feathers, garters, dance bustles, fans, staffs, weapons and pouches, all designed for show and to impress the onlooker.

In this style the most characteristic medium is hide or skin of the buffalo, elk, deer, antelope and other animals. This was either painted with various pigments applied with a porous bone brush or the surface was embroidered with quills or sewn with beads. Sometimes all three techniques were utilized together.

Embroidery with dyed porcupine or bird quills was widespread in early times but was later largely supplanted by beadwork. Among the first imported glass beads to find their way to the Plains area were of blue glass, traded by the Spanish, tiny seed beads and the larger pony beads in blue, black and white. At first, these glass beads were so scarce that they were sometimes used merely to outline quilled decoration. By the 1850's, however, they had largely replaced quillwork.

There are many overall similarities in Plains Indian art and, because of widespread trade and gift giving, it is sometimes difficult to determine the exact tribal origins of a specific object. Yet each of the various tribal groups developed distinctive stylistic or technological features and there are both subtle and obvious differences to be noted. Stylistically, three major regional divisions have been observed corresponding to the southern, central and northern Plains areas. In each of these regions distinctive decorative patterns, color preferences or emphasis on particular techniques were maintained.

Plains Indian art style emphasizes bold and colorful geometric patterns. Life forms which are somewhat rarer attempt to portray lively action but in a cursive, flat and stylized manner. It is often said that geometric patterning belonged to the women while life forms and depictive scenes were the work of the men. The men, however, apparently used both. Naturalistic designs are rarer than the geometric types and in some aspects may possibly be a later innovation taken over by the men. Towards the end of the 19th century when a great deal of Plains art was being made for commercial purposes, at least one woman is known to have painted the depictive scenes on muslin sheets.

Among the prevalent non-geometric forms are symbolic representations of supernatural human and animal figures such as the buffalo, bear, even insects and stars. Such motifs depicted the spiritual helper or guardian spirit which had appeared to an individual in a dream or vision and which was essential for his success and good health in life. These figures were painted on war shield covers as a means of magical protection, on robes and shirts, and on sacred medicine bundles to increase their spiritual power.

Plains sculpture, although primarily restricted to small and often utilitarian objects such as pipes, spoons and bowls, can be exceedingly fine. Pipe bowls of red or black soapstone were modeled into animal and human form, while the pipe stem bore relief figures, incised designs, cut-out work or inlay, and perhaps beading or quilling. The finest ornamentation was applied to pipes as well as other objects reserved for ceremonial occasions. Tobacco was

MAN'S BUCKSKIN SHIRT. Comanche, Southern Plains
(collected before 1900). 30″ x 61″; Gift of Mr. J. Z. Davis,
1896; #5119.

ritually smoked as a means to establish a connection with the supernatural.
Tobacco and ceremonial pipes were customarily a part of sacred medicine
bundles and were wrapped together with other objects of magical or sacred
significance which symbolized the vision encountered with the guardian spirit.
Among many Plains groups, the medicine bundle was regarded as an item of
wealth as well as a source of supernatural power.

The art tradition of the Plains Indians was allowed to flourish only for a
relatively brief time. In 1817, President James Monroe declared, "The hunter
or savage state requires a greater extent of territory to sustain it than is com-
patible with progress and the just claims of civilized life, and must yield to
it." He was referring to the Plains tribes and thus signaled the beginning of
a struggle which ended in the early 1880's when the last of the Indian peoples

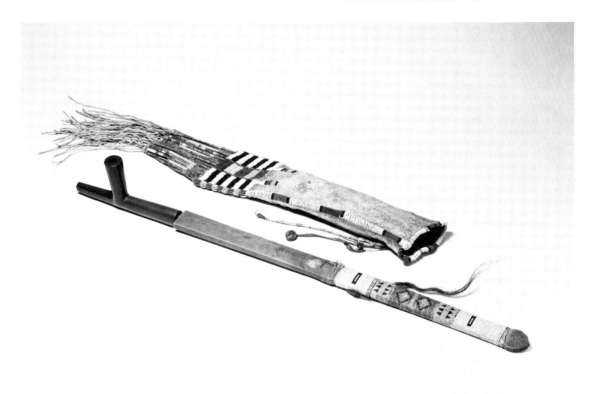

CEREMONIAL PIPE AND PIPE BAG. Lakota Sioux, Central Plains (collected before 1900). 34½″1.; 29″ x 4¾″; Gift of Mr. J. Z. Davis, 1896; #5209 A,B and 5207.

were forced on to reservations. Through a concerted effort on the part of the U.S. Government to slaughter the buffalo, the animal became virtually extinct by that time, removing from the Indians their principal food supply and reason for their nomadic way of life. In vain hopes of bringing back the buffalo and to resurrect the Indian dead who had been killed during the years of conflict with the whites, a religious revival known as the Ghost Dance spread among the surviving Plains groups. Participants in the revival wore Ghost Shirts made of coarse white cotton cloth, fringed and trimmed with eagle feathers. The upper portion of the garment was painted with vision symbols which acted as protective devices. It was believed that the person wearing the shirt was invulnerable to enemy bullets and therefore in this symbolic way revitalized the traditional status of the Plains warrior.

WOODEN FETISH. Crow, Central Plains (collected before 1900). 10¾″ x 2¾″; Gift of Dr. Joseph Simms, 1903; #23425.

COTTON GHOST DANCE SHIRT. Sioux, Central
Plains (collected before 1900). 27½″ x 58″; Gift of Mr. J. Z.
Davis, 1896; #5269.

Southwest
The artistic heritage of the Indians of the
Southwest can be traced back without interruption for over two thousand
years. Their art and artifacts have been found in a wide but relatively pre-
cise area, extending from southern Utah and Colorado across New Mexico
and Arizona into northern Mexico. The earliest inhabitants of this region
were not unlike their contemporaries elsewhere in the New World, sparse in
number and dependent upon hunting and food gathering for their livelihood.
Change came very slowly, but by at least 100 B.C., there were many small,
permanent villages whose residents were cultivating corn, squash, beans and

POTTERY WATER VESSEL. Acoma Pueblo, New Mexico (collected before 1900). 11″ x 7¼″; Purchased in 1903; #23367A.

cotton, domesticated plants which appear to have been introduced from Mesoamerica.

At this time too, the artists of the Southwest began to develop and elaborate the characteristic art forms of the region—pottery, textiles and fancy ornaments of shell and stone. Also, stylistic differences began to appear within the Southwestern tradition, indicating the emergence of several distinct cultural groups. Among them, the peoples of the high northern plateau where the Four Corners of New Mexico, Arizona, Utah and Colorado come together, have been given the collective name of Anasazi. The early Anasazi are known as Basketmakers. Their descendants, the Pueblo Indians, were the great architects of the Southwest, building large multiple-unit dwellings or "apartment houses" of finely wrought stone and adobe. Present-day Pueblo Indians are the Hopi, the Zuñi and the numerous Rio Grande peoples, some of whom still live in the ancient towns of their ancestors.

Traces of another prehistoric culture, the Mogollon, have been found in western New Mexico and eastern Arizona. Mogollen pottery, although showing influences from the Anasazi, is unique and among the finest in the early Southwest. The Hohokam, a third important group, settled along the Gila and Salt rivers in the deserts of southern Arizona. They cultivated the arid terrain by means of an intricate system of irrigation canals and waterways, built pyramids and ball courts and in a number of other ways appear to reflect the influence of Mesoamerican civilization.

The nature of this Mesoamerican relationship is still unclear but among the most interesting of recent discoveries is evidence for the close affiliation of the Hohokam and Mogollon to the ancient cultures of Chihuahua and Sonora in northern Mexico. Before 1000 A.D. the Southwesterners are believed to have settled in this Mexican region and to have built such towns as Casas Grandes. This was an important trading center in Chihuahua and copper bells and ornaments, exotic sea shells and tropical birds were among its main commercial items. We know that the birds, whose feathers were prized for ceremonial offerings, were kept in special houses with furnaces to heat them during the chilly desert nights.

Towards the end of the 13th century A.D. troublesome events began to occur in many parts of the Southwest. The Hohokam began to build great walled compounds for security against some still-unknown threat. Most of the large and handsome northern towns of the Anasazi were abandoned, some not without strife for their walls were left charred and burned and the inhabitants massacred. Other Pueblo communities found refuge in rough canyon lands where they built the famous "cliff dwellings," hidden and almost invulnerable. Drought, possibly internal conflict, and apparently the presence of alien groups along the northern borders of the Southwest combined to cause disruption among these once-peaceful peoples. The outsiders, nomadic Athapaskin hunters, were the ancestors of the modern Navaho and Apache. They settled in this area and gradually adopted many of the customs and arts of the earlier Southwestern peoples.

Pottery is one of the primary forms of Southwestern art. It first appeared about 100 B.C., continuing in importance as an artistic medium to the present. The finest of prehistoric Pueblo styles were developed after 900 A.D. and were based mainly upon the use of black and, later, black and red slips on a white ground with balanced yet extremely lively geometric designs. Even in the historic period, geometric motifs are favored and predominate in pottery design although frequently they are combined with European influenced floral, bird and animal patterns. Today, as in ancient times, each locality has its particularly distinctive style variations. Potters from the Rio Grande village of Acoma, for example, take pride in the technical superiority of their light, very thin-walled ceramics while the potters of Zuñi decorate their elegantly shaped vessels with delicate patterns of solid and hatched design areas.

The traditional sculpture of the Southwest is not widely known, perhaps because the majority of forms were associated with religious ritual and were kept hidden from the eyes of outsiders. For their shrines the Zuñi carved wooden images of the gods of war and music, and small stone animals or human figures were used as lucky pieces or placed on altars with prayer sticks and offerings of corn meal. These stone carvings are known as charms or "fetishes." Today, many of them are made for sale, but in the past, they were believed to contain a spiritual force which could come to the aid of the owner of the charm in time of need. The carver would initially select a stone for its color and unusual form and would shape out the little figure with considerable forcefulness of line and volume. Some examples are inlaid with coral, shell or turquoise, or beads, arrowpoints and feathers may be tied to the figure's back. Among the wide variety of these fetishes, the most common are those of the animals symbolic of the cardinal directions such as the eagle, bear and mountain lion, and others believed to be closely associated with the gods.

STONE CHARM IN SHAPE OF AN ANIMAL. Zuñi Pueblo,
New Mexico (collected before 1900). 1½″ x 3″; Collection M. H. de
Young Memorial Museum, 1895; #261.

Textiles were among the earliest arts of the Southwest. At first, a variety
of handwoven techniques such as twining and plaiting were applied to reeds,
yucca and other wild fibers, but about the beginning of our era, cotton began
to be used on a large "true" loom. Weaving among the prehistoric peoples of
the Southwest reached a climax of elegance and fine ornamentation about
1000 A.D. when colored yarns and a variety of techniques such as openwork

WOOL BLANKET. Navaho, New Mexico (collected before 1900).
46″ x 30″; Gift of Mr. J. Z. Davis, 1896; #5253.

became popular. The accounts of Coronado's first meeting with the Zuñi tell of receiving a peace offering of precious turquoise and cotton cloth, giving an idea of the value and significance of textiles among the early peoples of the Southwest.

The Spanish introduced sheep into this region and wool soon became an essential material for the weaver, especially for the production of the fine textiles of the Navaho. At the very end of the 17th century, the Navaho learned the skills of weaving from Pueblo groups who had taken refuge among them. Since that time, Navaho textiles have become widely and justly famous and, except for the Hopi, weaving has unfortunately all but ceased in the Pueblos. Early Navaho textiles reflect this Pueblo heritage with simple decoration of banded stripes, colored with natural wools, plant dyes, indigo and "bayeta" or the wool from unraveled trade cloth. Although early products of the Navaho looms were used for clothing, they became a much sought after trade item after 1870, and, before the turn of the century, were made primarily for the tourist trade. Navaho blankets, no longer used as clothing, were more thickly woven for use as rugs or wall coverings while the commercial yarns, bright aniline dyes and the traders who advised the weaver as to saleable patterns had a profound effect on style. A resurgence of interest in natural vegetable dyes and design innovations occurred in the 1920's and 1930's, resulting in the establishment of a wide range of new and quite interesting localized styles.

Jewelry making is another Southwestern art tradition which can be traced back to prehistoric times. Before the coming of the European, the materials most highly valued for the manufacture of beads, pendants, rings, bracelets and other ornaments were colorful sea shells imported from the Pacific coast and turquoise which was mined in various parts of the Southwest and northern Mexico. These materials were the focus of widespread trade in prehistoric times. In the 19th century, Mexicans introduced metal working techniques into the Southwest, first copper and brass working, then silversmithing. The Navaho first practiced the craft, later the Zuñi and various other Pueblo communities. Navaho work is stark and heavy, patterns are simple and traditional. The silver itself is emphasized while the inlaid turquoise stones are few but large and significant in the design. In contrast, Pueblo silver jewelry is more ornate and characteristically built up of small colorful mosaic units, composed of white, pink and red shell, coral and jet, along with the traditional turquoise.

SILVER AND TURQUOISE NECKLACE AND BRACELET.
Navaho, New Mexico. 14¼″ length and 2⅞″ diameter, respectively;
Gift of the Estate of Margaret Post Stark; #71.23.3 and 71.23.7.

California and the Far West

In 1602, three Spanish galleons set out from Acapulco, Mexico, venturing northwest along the Pacific to unknown regions, searching for a "rich and populous city named Quivara." The Spaniards found no traces of the mythical city but Fray Antonio de la Ascension, the geographer of the expedition, described the land they finally discovered as "an island, very near to the terrestrial paradise" and, in amazement he wrote of "the grandeur, length and width of this Kingdom of the Californias, the many people there, and their docility."* Since the expedition had returned with no rich treasure, few, except the Franciscan monks who built their missions up and down the California coast, listened to these praises, and the Far West was left peacefully to its original Indian inhabitants for another two hundred years.

Although California was not an island, Fray Antonio's description fitted the California coast with its gentle climate, fertile valleys and its rich forests and seashore. He did not venture inland, however, where beyond the ranges of the Sierra Nevada the warming, humid effect of the Pacific Ocean diminishes and the earth is not so generous with nature's bounty.

Other parts of the Far West are quite different from the Pacific coastal plain. The Great Basin lands of Nevada and Utah form the high desert, dry in the summer and very cold in winter. North of this area, between the Cascade and Rocky Mountains, is a high plateau country of deep forests and icy rivers. Nomadic hunting bands had penetrated these areas as early as 10,000 B.C. in search of wandering herds of big game animals. They left only slight traces of their passage.

Somewhat later in time, as an evermore sophisticated technology was developed to deal with the environment, permanent groups of foragers made the Far West their home. These people camped where they found food and water, sometimes using caves for shelter. They generally set up an "annual round" returning to the same sites year after year. Stone tools for both hunting and for the grinding of seeds are found in the camp sites of this period. In

---

* "Father Antonio de la Ascension's account of the voyage of Sebastian Vizcano." Reprinted in translation in: Henry R. Wagner, *Spanish Voyages to the Northwest Coast of America.*

dry caves, even more perishable objects of wood and fiber have been preserved. From this evidence we know that these prehistoric nomadic groups slept on beds of grass, dressed in fiber aprons, sandals, and skin robes, that they used shell ornaments, and they made various types of basketry for cooking and gleening. They also practiced some kinds of rituals, perhaps curing rites, using deer hoof rattles, bone whistles and what appear to be medicine bags.

In California, where food was far more abundant than in the Plateau and Great Basin, there was less necessity for continual wandering. Beginning about 200 B.C. people started living in permanent villages. These settlements gradually increased in both size and number, and by contact times the population density of California had become greater than that of any other part of prehistoric North America.

In each of the regions of the Far West, Indian peoples came to a basically similar way of life. All were food gatherers, collecting seeds, roots (acorns in California), or, when possible, fishing and hunting for whatever products nature made available. Some groups did borrow traits or techniques from Indian neighbors on the fringes of the Far West, but these borrowings were few and had little effect on the general cultural patterns as a whole. In southern California, for example, some of the techniques for farming and pottery making were learned from the peoples of the Southwest. In the Plateau and in northern California, the importance of a man's wealth and rank were ideas borrowed from the peoples of the Northwest Coast. On the eastern edge of the Great Basin and the Plateau, tribes which had acquired horses after the arrival of the Europeans, also adopted certain customs of the Plains Indians.

The art of the Far West was generally restricted to the ornamentation of such useful objects as baskets and tools, and to the creation of ornaments and costume for ceremonial and everyday wear. From an early time on, the techniques, the forms, and the styles of Far Western art began to take on some of the characteristics to be seen among the historic tribes. Beads, charms and ornaments of irridescent abalone and other shell, stone and incised bone, basketry, feather work, chipped obsidian implements and decorated steatite pipes are found among the burial offerings of the early peoples. Large numbers of ground and polished charmstones occur in sites throughout the area, while carved steatite effigies representing sea creatures, some of them encrusted with shell decoration, are unique to the southern California coast.

Nevertheless, within the total range of art production, the real strength of Far Western art is in basketry. For the most part, there was no knowledge of (or perhaps disinterest in) pottery making. Instead, baskets were used as containers, for carrying, cooking and storage, for cradles and hats, and even as ceremonial gifts and ornaments.

In each tribe or region, special basketry techniques were favored. Northern peoples are said to have used only twining, the central groups practiced twining as well as coiling and other techniques, while in the south, basketmakers utilized the coiling method to the near exclusion of others. Methods of decoration also varied by area. In the north, ornamentation was only applied to a basket by a facing. This means that the primary structure served as a foundation and the decorative elements were introduced either by a false embroidery or by wrapping the twined elements with colored fibers. In contrast, the southern and central California peoples used a wide range of decorative techniques. Even though the availability of different colored grasses and fibers determined the basic style in each region, there was room for surprising originality.

Two tribal groups, the Pomo of central California and the Washo of the California-Nevada border region near Lake Tahoe, are credited with making some of the finest of the Far Western baskets. The Pomo occupied the valley of the Russian River and the basin of Clear Lake in the coastal ranges to the north of San Francisco Bay. Their basketry is unique in the number of techniques employed and in the elaboration of decorative additions applied to it. The fancy baskets were made by the coiling method and many were decorated with brilliant mosaics of feathers, beads, and shells. Bright scarlet from woodpecker scalps, black from quail plumes, and yellow from the meadow lark were the common colors utilized to form the design patterns. These feather baskets were often further elaborated by rows of shell beads or dangling pendants. All of this color and textural variation combined to form a truly radiant image. The most elaborate baskets, along with more restrained but incredibly finely woven ones—many Pomo baskets have 60 stitches to the inch, while others are tiny miniatures rather than normal in size—were regarded as personal treasures. They were used as gifts, often in marriage exchange, or they were ritually destroyed in honor of the dead.

Washo basketry, on the other hand, is refined and even restrained in decorative technique. The fancy pieces are spherical, small-mouthed baskets called *degikup*. They are invariably coiled on a three-rod foundation of wil-

FEATHER GIFT BASKET. Pomo, Mendocino County, California
(collected before 1900). 3½″ x 11¾″; Purchased in 1902; #21470.

MINIATURE BASKETS WITH LIGHTNING, STAR, AND
DOUBLE ARROW DESIGNS. Pomo, Mendocino County, California. 4″ to ½″ diameter; Gift of Mrs. H. Welsh, 1924; #51972A-J.

BOTTLE-NECK BASKET. Yokut, Tulare County, California. 4¼″ x 2½″; Gift of Mrs. H. Welsh, 1924; #51960B.

COOKING BASKET. Washoe, Alpine County, California. 6¼″ x 6½″; Lent Anonymously, 1921; #L9114.

low, using fern root, water birch, and redbud for the patterns. While the stitching is never so fine as that of the Pomo, the subtle use of design pattern and color, along with the evenness of the finish make Washo basketry outstanding. The most famous of the Washo basket makers was a woman named Louisa Keyser. Using the nickname Dat-So-La-Lee, and with the help of an agent who registered and advertised her work, she received fees of several thousand dollars per basket, many of which were sold at the St. Louis Arts and Crafts Industrial Exposition which she attended in 1919.

Northwest Coast

This rainy, forested strip of coastline extending from southern Alaska to northern Oregon is a rugged area of mountains, fjords and inlets. Its Indian inhabitants were divided into several different tribal groups but their rich cultural and artistic traditions were basically similar. They were fishermen, hunters, and gatherers; and the forest animals, the sea creatures and their spirit counterparts make up the primary motif, theme and symbolism of Northwest Coast art.

These animal motifs were combined with the human figure, reflecting a significant aspect of Northwest Coast religion and mythology. It was thought that beneath the external zoomorphic shape of different animals could be found a man-like supernatural who could speak intelligibly and had the motives and desires of a human being. From time to time these forest and sea spirits bestowed some of their powers upon deserving humans. The individual would be magically possessed by the spirit who taught him new dances and ritual, gave him specific property rights or in some way increased his wealth and status. A significant theme expressed in Northwest Coast art was man's encounter with these supernatural beings and the benefits derived this way for the individual, his clan or community. In some instances the mythical being was thought to have taken human shape and to have founded the clan lineage itself. The symbolic representation of such mythical encounters constituted the clan crest or device which was proudly displayed in painted and sculptured forms.

Wealth, status and the importance of a person's rank and ancestral lineage were of major concern in the Northwest Coast. To attest to this status and importance, clan crests and symbols of rank were displayed wherever possible—from small, delicately carved feast spoons to grandiose totem poles

MAN INSIDE A FISH. Possibly Tlingit, Northwest Coast.
12½″ x 4″; Gift of Mrs. E. Martin, 1910; #37764B.

FOOD DISH IN THE SHAPE OF A FROG. Kwakiutl,
Northwest Coast (collected before 1900). 11½″ x 6″; Dr. H.
W. Yemans, 1897; #6328.

WOODEN FEAST BOWL. Kwakiutl, Northwest Coast (collected before 1900). 30" x 44" x 25"; Gift of Mr. John Bardwell, 1887; #5751.

and houseposts. The totem pole appears to have been a relatively recent innovation in Northwest Coast art. Carved with crest devices and symbolizing important events in the clan's history it was erected outside the dwelling to announce to visitors the social status of the members of the household. Prominent families set up the finest poles they could afford, hoping to shame passersby of lesser rank. Carved houseposts, which appear to have gained artistic importance before totem poles, stood inside the house as roof beam supports. These monumental pole and post carvings were brilliantly painted and refurbished for ceremonial events.

For important occasions such as house building, marriages, the birth of a noble child, or the funerary rites of a chief, feasts known as potlatches were held and many works of art were made to be displayed or given away to the assembled guests. The potlatch was an important and colorful event. Hosts and guests dressed in their finest garments and carried staffs or other paraphernalia—this rich attire displaying the crest and individual rank of the wearer. The interior of the clan house was decorated with carved feast dishes, figure sculpture and painted screens or house boards, and filled with piles of blankets, stacks of decorated boxes and other valuables to be given to the guests. Assembled according to rank, the hosts and guests feasted on fish oil and other delicacies, watched masked dancers perform and heard the orations

FIGURE OF DANCING SHAMAN. Haida, Northwest
Coast (collected before 1900). 24″ x 8½″; source unknown;
#180-97.

CHIEF'S STAFF. Tlingit, Northwest Coast, 36⅜″ x 4″;
Gift of Mr. Hermann Schussler, 1919; #45201.

IVORY AND BONE SHAMAN'S CHARMS (Depictions of Octopus, Killer Whale and Wolf). Probably Tlingit, Northwest Coast. 4″ to 6″; Gifts of Thomas Bishop, 1909, and Hermann Schussler, 1919; #2898L.A.-D., 45189A&B, 45191.

SHAMAN'S GUARDIAN FIGURE. Possibly Kwakiutl, Northwest Coast. 9″ x 2½″; Gift of Captain William Noyes, 1905; #25826.

IVORY NEEDLE CASE. Tlingit, Northwest Coast (collected before 1900). 6″ x ½″; Gift of Dr. H. W. Yemans, 1897; #6342.

CONTAINER CARVED OF HORN. Northwest Coast (collected before 1900). 3½″ x 1″; Gift of Dr. H. W. Yemans, 1897; #6343.

of the high-ranking chiefs proclaiming the rights and status given to them by the supernatural.

In the Northwest Coast certain of the supernatural or mythical beings portrayed in art were considered to be personal guardian spirits. A particular guardian spirit could be inherited through the clan lineage or, through trances, purificatory rites and vision quests, an individual himself might experience spirit possession. Some spirits were thought to aid in the curing of disease. The person in contact with such supernaturals were the shamans or curers of the community. To work a cure the shaman performed specific rituals to control the supernatural and as he worked over the patient with rattles and carved ivory tubes, he would sometimes wrestle with the invisible spirit to subdue it. Strung on a necklace around his neck or sewn to his dance apron were a variety of beautifully carved ivory or bone charms representing the particular animal supernaturals with which he communicated. The shaman was sometimes portrayed in art as a wooden doll-like figure with shaggy hair and special costume or with small figures at each side, possibly representing his assistants.

The shaman may have carved some of his magical equipment himself, but in the Northwest Coast not everyone could be an artist. Standards of artistic perfection were high and sculptors learned the techniques and the rituals associated with their work through a period of apprenticeship to an established master carver. The reputation of a talented artist and superb craftsman spread far and wide and he received commissions from the wealthiest chiefs. The artist's tools were simple although beautifully made and were often decorated with carving. The basic wood-working implements were the elbow adze and the D-shaped adze—both fitted with stone, bone or shell

WOOD AND HAIR PAINT BRUSH. Northwest Coast (collected before 1900). 12″ x ¾″; Gift of Dr. H. W. Yemans, 1897; #6314.

ARGILLITE PIPE. Haida, Northwest Coast. 9½″ x 3″;
Gift of Mrs. E. Peterson, 1917; #42369.

blades in prehistoric times, later with metal blades obtained through trade.
Sharp animal teeth such as those of the beaver were used as knives for cutting
and incising and finished carvings were smoothed with rough, dried fish skin
in place of sandpaper. The Northwest Coast Indian artist used a wide variety
of materials such as cedar bark, fur, leather, hair, copper, bone, teeth and
iridescent sea shell to enrich his work but paint was among the most important of embellishments, giving volume and definition to his carving. Before
commercial paints were readily available, plant and earth colors were used. A
characteristic blue green was obtained from clays and copper oxide, shells
were made into white pigments, black made from charcoal, reds and yellows
from minerals, tree bark, plants and berries. Colors were mixed with fish oil
and painted on the object with brushes which were themselves often decorated with fine carving.

European contact initially spurred increased artistic efforts among the
Indians of the Northwest Coast. The wealth acquired through the fur trade
made art available to a wider group of patrons and new trade materials, particularly metal tools, made the production of sculpture quicker and easier. The
Indian artists soon found that some of their work was readily bought up by
white traders. The Haida, for example, began making small pipes, plates and
miniature totem poles and other carvings in shiny black slate or argillite.
Early examples of this stone carving bear some resemblance to the style of
the Yankee sailor's scrimshaw, but later specimens are closer to other Northwest Coast art forms.

Eskimo

In the far north, the tree line separating the barren Arctic tundra from the coniferous forests further to the south generally marks the boundary between Indian and Eskimo territory. The Eskimo, who are distinct from the Indian, live in the coastal regions from southern Alaska to the Arctic Sea and eastward to Labrador and Greenland.

A hardy and inventive people, the Eskimo were faced with the constant struggle against the Arctic winters which dominate much of the year and bring icy winds, sub-zero temperatures and the dim twilight of the northern latitudes. They are relatively recent immigrants to the New World, having apparently migrated from the Siberian Arctic sometime during the second or third millennium B.C. Archaeologists have determined that the early ancestors of the Eskimo first established their villages along the coasts of the Bering and Chuckchi Seas. As are their descendants, the prehistoric Eskimo were hunters, especially of the sea mammals such as the walrus, seal and whale. They utilized whatever material was available in their harsh environment and with such innovations as the toboggan, skin boat, sled and toggle harpoon, they made existence and livelihood in the Arctic more efficient and dependable.

Despite the dangers and difficulties of life in the far north, both the ancient and modern Eskimo delighted in art. Their art is not of monumental size nor is it elaborate in style. Since raw materials were scarce, much of Eskimo art is devoted to the ornamentation of every day useful objects such as tools, combs, trinket boxes, weapons and pipes. Most characteristic are small, realistically rendered carvings of animals or human figures in ivory, bone and wood or implements and pipes in these same materials engraved with scenes from Eskimo life or myth.

Ivory was the artist's favorite material, especially walrus ivory and the dark fossil tusks of paleolithic elephants—when they could be obtained. The ivory was seasoned and dried to prevent cracking and stripped of its rough outer surface with an adze. The bow drill and awl were used to section the ivory and short curved metal blades or gravers, mounted in wood or ivory handles, were used for incising fine lines and details.

WOODEN MASK OF BIRD. Eskimo, south of Norton
Sound, Alaska. 7½″ x 10⅞″; Gift of Mrs. H. B. Hughes,
1926; #53353B.

IVORY CRIBBAGE BOARD. Eskimo, Alaska. 20″ x 2½″;
Gift of Mrs. H. B. Hughes, 1926; #53354B.

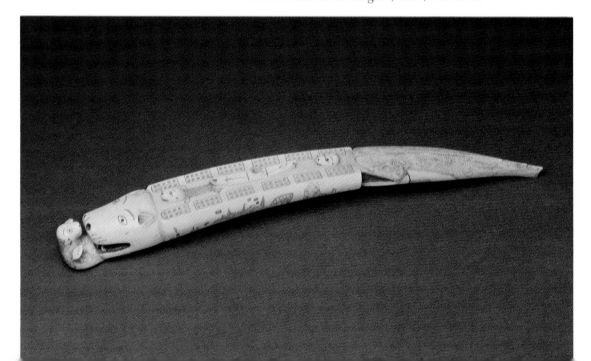

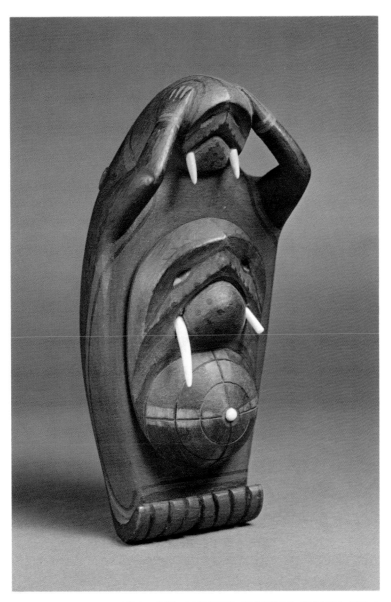

WOODEN TRINKET BOX CARVED IN THE SHAPE OF A
WALRUS. Eskimo, Southern Alaska. 8½″ x 3⅝″; Gift of Mr. William Gerstle, 1907; #26662.

WOODEN MASK. Eskimo, Bering Sea Coast, Alaska. 23″ x 23″; Lent by Mr. and Mrs. Philip McCoy; #71.23.

Masks are perhaps an even better known aspect of Eskimo art than are the engravings. Masks are constructed mainly of wood—usually driftwood—and with skin, ivory, fur, baleen and a variety of other materials added for details. Such masks were to be found primarily among the Alaskan Eskimo. They were worn during festivals and dances which were believed to bring the supernatural into closer contact with human beings in order to insure the continued welfare of the community. In their fantastic and symbolic forms were depicted the world of the supernatural, the sun and moon deities, the animals which man depended upon for food, and a range of good and evil spirits which inhabited the rocks and crannies of the earth. Many masks represented the shaman's tutelary spirits who helped him to see into the future or travel to the world of the supernatural seeking the lost souls of the sick. In Eskimo society, the shaman or curer was most frequently the visionary who saw the form of the spirit and translated it into the concrete shape of the mask. Thus, the mask both represented and opened a way to the supernatural world where mortals might find solution to the difficult problems of finding food and shelter or staving off disease and discomfort which accompanied the difficult Arctic life.

MESOAMERICA
AND THE
CENTRAL ANDES

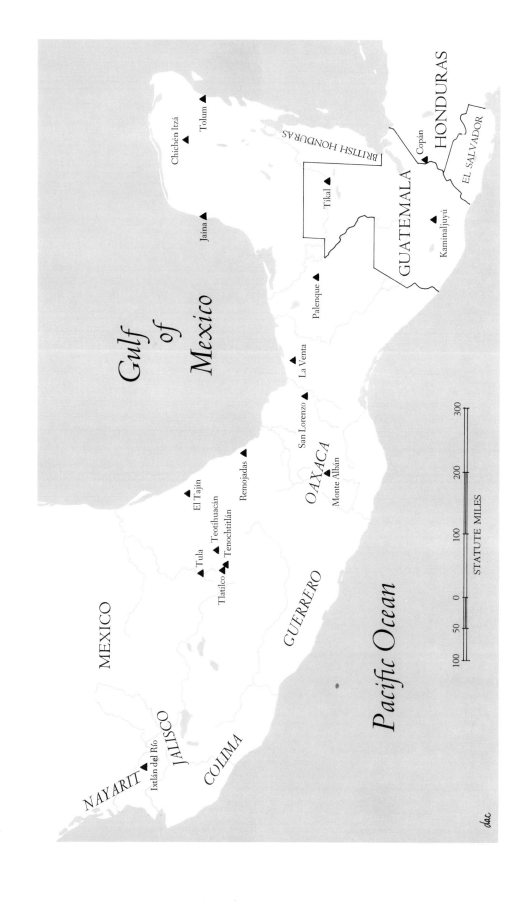

Gulf of Mexico

Pacific Ocean

MEXICO

NAYARIT

Ixtlán del Río ▲

JALISCO

COLIMA

GUERRERO

OAXACA

Monte Albán ▲

San Lorenzo ▲

La Venta ▲

Remojadas ▲

Tlatilco ▲
Teotihuacán ▲
Tenochtitlán ▲▲

Tula ▲

El Tajín ▲

Jaina ▲

Palenque ▲

Chichén Itzá ▲

Tolum ▲

Tikal ▲

Kaminaljuyú ▲

Copán ▲

GUATEMALA

BRITISH HONDURAS

HONDURAS

EL SALVADOR

100 50 0 100 200 300
STATUTE MILES

dac

MESOAMERICA

Period (dates)	Western Mexico	Central Highlands	Oaxaca	Gulf Coast	Maya Lowlands North	Maya Lowlands South
Late Postclassic —1500	Tarascan Empire	Aztec	Mitla	IV / III Cempoala	Mayapán	
Early Postclassic —900	Amapa (various figurine styles)	Tula	Monte Alban IV	Cempoala II / I — Cerro de las Mesas	Toltec Chichén	
Late Classic	Aztatlan; Chametla	Teotihuacán IV	Monte Alban IIIB	El Tajín — Cerro de las Mesas	Rio-Bec	Petén Maya — Tepeu
Early Classic —300	Mezcala	Teotihuacán III	Monte Alban IIIA	Upper Tres Zapotes — Upper Remojadas II	Yaxuná Chicanel	Tzakol — Holmul
Late Preclassic A.D. 0 B.C. —300	?	Teotihuacán II — Teotihuacán I	Monte Alban II	Middle Tres Zapotes — Upper Remojadas I — Cerro de las Mesas	Dzibilchaltún	
Middle Preclassic —900	Chupícuaro — San Isidro	Cuicuilco — Ticoman	Monte Alban I — Tlatilco Zacatenco	Tres Zapotes — Lower Remojadas		Mamon
Early Preclassic —1500	Marcelia — ?	Ixtapaluca		La Venta — San Lorenzo		
Incipient Cultivation —2100	Pox Pottery					

PERU

Period (dates)	Coast North Inca	Coast Central Inca	Coast South Inca	Sierra South Inca	Sierra Central Inca	Sierra North Inca
Late Horizon —1500	Inca	Inca	Inca	Inca	Inca	Inca
Late Intermediate Period —900	Chimu	Chancay — Pachacamac	Ica	Early Inca (Killke)	Chupachu	Cajamarca
Middle Horizon	Tiahuanaco Influence			Huari (influence)		(influence)
Early Intermediate Period A.D. 0 B.C. —300	Moche — Gallinazo Miramar (Vicus) — Salinar	Lima	Nasca	Local Styles — Pucara	Kotosh Higueras	Recuay
Early Horizon —900	Tembladera — Cupisnique (Chavín Influence)	Ancon	Paracas	Chanapata — Qaluyu Maravalle	Kotosh Chavín	Chavín
Initial Period —1500		Haldas		Erizo	Kotosh Mito	
	La Florida — Chuquitanta					
Incipient Cultivation —2100	Huaca Prieta					

Mesoamerica

The amazement and disbelief of Cortéz and his conquering army when they at last reached Tenochtitlán, the capital of the Aztecs, is contained in the remarkable Chronicles of Bernal Díaz del Castillo. Upon entering the Valley of Mexico he recorded that, "when we saw so many cities and villages built in the water of the lake, and other great towns on dry land, and that straight and level causeway going towards Mexico, we were all amazed and said that it was like the enchantments they tell of in the legends of Amadis on account of the great towers and cues and buildings rising from the water."* Tenochtitlán was truly an impressive sight with its gleaming white pyramids and temples, its bustling markets, broad avenues and canals. It was the capital of a vast empire which dominated a region from the Gulf coast to the western mountains of the Tarascan kingdom and south to the frontiers of present-day Guatemala.

Cortéz entered the city in 1519, and by the end of the 16th century the Aztec empire had vanished and none of Tenochtitlán's awesome pyramids and monuments were left standing. The Aztec empire belonged to the brief, final epoch of Mesoamerican prehistory. Although the Spanish could not have realized it, the magnificence of Tenochtitlán had its foundations in the splendors of earlier civilizations whose story—their society, religion and art, their growth and downfall—has only been revealed by archaeology.

Archaeologists use the term Mesoamerica to refer to the area of central and southern Mexico, Guatemala, El Salvador and parts of Honduras where complex societies flourished at or before the arrival of the first Europeans. This is a region of great natural contrasts and beauty. In the highlands of Mexico and Guatemala distinct civilizations flourished and interacted, and great cities were built and then destroyed throughout the later phases of Mesoamerican prehistory. In the east, in the lands of the Olmec, the Maya and the Huastec, somber, humid rain forest covers the broad flat alluvial plain bordering the Gulf of Mexico and the Caribbean. Here, a different style of complex society developed. It was focused upon awesome "ceremonial" precincts with elaborate temples and public architecture, built and maintained by widespread populations and administered by specialist priests and bureaucrats. On the west coast of Mexico, where only a narrow strip of coastal plain runs for most of the length of the Pacific shore, a third and distinctive area of cultural and artistic orientation developed. This area, separated from cen-

---

* Bernal Díaz del Castillo, *The True History of the Conquest of New Spain.*

tral Mexico by rugged mountain terrain, was relatively unaffected by the political crises which continually shook the central and eastern areas of Mesoamerica. A good deal more archaeological field work will be needed before we can successfully relate the cultural developments of this western zone with the mainstream of Mesoamerican culture history.

THE PRECLASSIC PERIOD   After long centuries of hunting and gathering, settled village life and agricultural production became the dominant mode of human adaptation to the Mesoamerican environment. At this time pottery vessels and figurines began to be produced. This ceramic art becomes the archaeologist's key to both the chronolgy and the definition of these early cultures. In central Mexico early vessels were slipped and fired to a deep red, brown or black and modelled into bowls or jars with graceful high necks or stirrup spouts. They were then geometrically incised and burnished to a rich luster. Pottery was also used for little round masks, figurines and musical instruments such as tamborines and whistles. These objects, carefully buried with the dead, show a developing religious ceremonialism and a belief in

POTTERY MASK. Tlatilco, Valley of Mexico. Middle Preclassic. 4¾″ x 5¾″; Lent by the Foundation for the Preservation of American Pre-History; #L71.-2.66.

CLAY FIGURINE. Tlatilco, Valley of Mexico. Middle Preclassic. 5¼″ x 2″; Lent by the Foundation for the Preservation of American Pre-History; #L71.2.18.

STONE WERE-JAGUAR FIGURE. Olmec, Veracruz, Mexico. Early Preclassic. 12½″ x 7½″; Bequest of Mr. Bruno Adriani; #L71.-15.35.

SERPENTINE MASK. Xochipala, Guerrero, Mexico. Early Preclassic. 4⅛″ x 5¾″; Salinger Trust Fund; #72.43.

some form of after life. The figurines may also have had significance in fertility rites for many of them portray females with sensuous bodies and enormously fat legs. A number of other figures are amusingly life-like, depicting acrobats, dancers, musicians, masked figures, dwarfs and even two-headed monsters. They provide an interesting and significant insight into the life of the preclassic village peoples.

The earliest great art style, and one which was spread over large areas of Mesoamerica, is called Olmec. The hallmark of this style is the elaborate and sensitive carving of stone, especially jadite and other green stone, and the characteristic motif of the so-called were-jaguar, part man, part feline, with a puffy downturned mouth and infantile human facial features. Small Olmec style objects have been found in central and western Mexico, but the Olmec heartland seems to have been in the lowlands of the Gulf Coast in southern Veracruz and Tabasco. Here, one finds the large Olmec stone sculpture and planned ceremonial centers. The best known architectural complexes are at San Lorenzo in Veracruz and La Venta in Tabasco where large mounds and plazas are complemented by carved stelae, altars and the famous colossal stone heads. Great blocks of basalt for these sculptures—some weighing up to 20 tons—were transported from the distant Tuxla Mountains to the ceremonial sites at a tremendous expenditure of human energy.

Olmec culture seems to have flourished on the Gulf Coast from around 1200 to 500 B.C. Even before the terminal date there were signs of trouble within the ongoing Olmec culture, for many of the stone sculptures at San Lorenzo were mutilated and the site itself was abandoned around 900 B.C. La Venta continued to be maintained and received offerings through 500 B.C., then it too was mysteriously abandoned and the Olmecs and their peculiar art style disappeared.

Olmec influence on the rest of Mesoamerica must have been significant. There is evidence that the Olmec first used the bar and dot numerical notation system and perhaps the calendar system which was eventually adopted throughout Mesoamerica. While we do not know the full extent of their influence on later cultures, or the degree of control they exercised over their contemporaries, the widespread occurrence of Olmec style artifacts does indicate an intricate trade network which covered much of Mesoamerica at a very early date.

THE CLASSIC PERIOD   Archaeologists have long argued about temporal versus developmental sequence to provide a framework for the outlining of culture history. The "Classic Period" implies the fullest development of aboriginal culture, although in Mesoamerica, this fluorescence took place in different areas at different times. Current usage dictates an arbitrary time

POTTERY VESSEL. Maya, N.E. Guatemala. Late Preclassic. 5″ x 8⅜″; Gift of Dr. Ernest Forbes, 1933; #54341.

MONTE ALBAN, ZAPOTEC CEREMONIAL CEN-
TER. Oaxaca, Mexico. Photo by J. P. Dwyer.

period of six hundred years (300 to 900 A.D.) to be called the Classic Period. This arbitrary time period is more or less fixed by the earliest and latest dated stelae from the Maya area, and does, in fact, indicate the fluorescence of that culture.

Maya civilization, centered in the lowland tropical forests of the Guatemalan Peten region and neighboring Chiapas, Mexico, produced some of the most remarkable art and architecture in Mesoamerica. Their art can be conveniently divided into two aspects. The first comprises architectural ornamentation including stone and stucco relief, carved wooden lintels and wall paintings, as well as the free-standing stone sculptures, stelae and altars. This type of art is best seen at the archaeological sites where it forms a part of the overall impression of the Maya center. The second aspect of Maya art is the small portable sculpture and pottery usually associated with burials or other kinds of religious offerings. The Maya were fine workers of jade, obsidian and shell using these materials for body ornaments such as ear spools, beads, and masks. These ornaments were also included in grave offerings.

Outside of the Maya area a number of other events were taking place which would shape the course of the future cultural history of the whole of Mesoamerica. The most important of these developments was the emergence of central Mexico as a dominant political power surrounded by independent and important regional centers of varying strengths. This political pattern continued until the time of the Spanish conquest when independent kingdoms, resentful of the power and domination of the central Mexican Aztec state, aided the Europeans.

STONE FIGURE. Teotihuacán, Mexico. Early Classic. 9" x 5"; Bequest of Mr. Bruno Adriani; #L71.15.6.

One important condition of the Classic Period in central Mexico was the rise of urbanism as a settlement system. There is little doubt that the most important urban center to develop in prehistoric Mesoamerica was the great city of Teotihuacán located in the northeast corner of the Valley of Mexico. The ruins of this once great city are today, as they were in Aztec times, an important place of pilgrimage where visitors wonder at the splendor that once existed.

Teotihuacán's ascendency began prior to the Classic Period proper. The initial settlement and constructions at Teotihuacán began in the last few centuries before the beginning of the Christian era. The site gradually increased in size and importance until about 300 A.D., the city had reached its greatest expansion and its influence was being felt as far away as highland Guatemala. At its height Teotihuacán covered eight square miles with a population estimated at 125,000 or more inhabitants. The plan of the city followed a rectangular grid and a broad avenue, now called the "street of the dead," stretched for two miles, flanked by pyramids, platforms, palaces, and great ceremonial enclosures.

The art of Teotihuacán is distinctive and its widespread occurrence at sites distant from central Mexico indicates the influence and importance of this urban center. Although Teotihuacán produced little monumental stone sculpture, enormous quantities of pottery of distinctive shape and decoration were apparently manufactured at this site and traded over much of Mesoamerica. One of the characteristic Teotihuacán pottery shapes is the cylinder jar with tripod slab feet, the body of the vessel often decorated with painted stucco. A characteristic art form at Teotihuacán was wall painting. Numerous elaborately painted wall frescos have been uncovered by archaeologists working at the site. It is evident from the well-preserved murals that all of the later major Mesoamerican deities were known and being depicted in Teotihuacán times.

The elegance of the Maya and the brilliance of the Teotihuacán were not unrivalled by other Classic Period cultures elsewhere in Mesoamerica. Perhaps the most important of these was at Monte Albán, located on a high promontory overlooking the fertile valley of Oaxaca. About 500 B.C. or perhaps earlier, the architects of Monte Albán began to level the mountain

POTTERY URN OF THE GOD *COCIJO*. Monte Albán, Oaxaca, Mexico. Late Classic. 14½″ x 14½″; Gift of Dr. Ernest Forbes, 1933; #54431.

POTTERY URN OF OLD MAN GOD "5F". Monte Albán, Oaxaca, Mexico. Late Classic. 7⅞″ x 7½″; Gift of Dr. Ernest Forbes, 1933; #54376.

ALABASTER VASE IN FORM OF A MONKEY. Veracruz, Mexico. Post Classic. 7″ x 5″; Bequest of Mr. Bruno Adriani; #L71.15.39.

POTTERY CUP IN THE FORM OF A HEAD. Remojadas, Veracruz, Mexico. Early Classic. 5½″ x 5¼″; Gift of Mr. Herbert Fleishhacker, 1935; #54761.

top to make way for temples, plazas and pyramids. At first, these structures were relatively unambitious in size but unique in their sculptural decoration. As time passed they became more elaborate, and by the Classic Period, Monte Albán was a very large site consisting of numerous buildings around plazas in a well planned display of visual regularity. Long low structures alternated with higher more impressive ones, each with a wide stairway leading down to a plaza. Monte Albán seems to have been ceremonial or civic rather than an urban center, but only more excavation on the slopes around the major structures will resolve the question of population density at the site.

Monte Albán was also a necropolis, and the tombs of important priests or officials were decorated with murals depicting the primary gods of an enormous pantheon. The art style and the religious themes relate the murals to the Zapotec people as described by the Spanish in the sixteenth century, and it is fairly certain that the modern Zapotec Indians of Oaxaca are the direct descendants of the builders of Monte Albán. Many of the subterranean tombs also contained funerary offerings including the famous clay urns depicting various Zapotec deities. Interestingly, the richest tomb at the site, Tomb 7, contained a treasure of gold and precious stones worked in the Mixtec style. This tomb, which was excavated in 1931 and 1932 by the Mexican archaeologist Alfonso Caso, seems to indicate a foreign presence at Monte Albán. Caso concluded that in the Post Classic Period, the Zapotecs abandoned the site and the Mixtecs, coming down from the north cleaned out an ancient tomb in order to reuse it for the burial of some important person.

STONE CELT. Mezcala, Guerrero, Mexico. Early Classic. 2½″ x 6½″; Bequest of Mr. Bruno Adriani; #L71.15.20.

POTTERY FIGURE. Remojadas, Veracruz, Mexico. Early Classic. 17″ x 14″; Gift of Mr. Dudley Gunn; #60.3.

STONE HACHA SHOWING A BENT LEG. Central Veracruz, Mexico. Classic. 15½" x 9½"; Bequest of Mr. Bruno Adriani; #L71.15.16.

POTTERY DOG. Colima, Western Mexico. Classic. 14½" x 6½"; Gift of M. H. de Young; #42.16.

STONE YOKE WITH
THREE FACES. Central
Veracruz, Mexico. Classic.
17½" x 15"; Bequest of Mr.
Bruno Adriani; #L71.15.36.

A number of different cultures flourished along the Gulf Coast. Although they all had their distinctive beginnings in earlier Preclassic developments, the Classic Period brought the strong influences of Teotihuacán and the Maya which spurred more elaborate and monumental artistic efforts. In central Veracruz, the Remojadas culture is famed for its ceramic sculptures—unusually sensitive clay figures of men and women, warriors, dancing boys and girls, and the well-known Smiling Head deities. Preclassic varieties were small but with the passing centuries the Remojadas artists became bolder, and in Classic times much larger figures were made, some almost life size. All were clearly and carefully modelled—the earlier ones by hand, later examples usually in molds—giving a glimpse of the activities of these ancient peoples, how they dressed and their particular modes of personal decoration.

Further to the north, but still on the Gulf Coast, the art of a people known as the Classic Veracruz civilization stands midway between the realistic and exuberant, curvilinear styles of the Maya and the contrasting severe forms of Teotihuacán. The center of this culture appears to have been the imposing site of El Tajín with its ornate architecture and numerous ball courts. El Tajín is located in an area of dense vegetation and the site itself has not been completely explored. It is most famous for its Pyramid of the Niches, an elaborate structure of stepped architectural elaboration with 365 ornamental niches and decoration of carved stone relief panels. Much of our information about the Mesoamerican ceremonial ball game comes from relief carvings found at El Tajín. It was played in a specially constructed court with sloping walls along side of a rectangular playing field. Similar ball courts are found at most major Mesoamerican sites from the Classic Period on. The game itself was played with a rubber ball by teams of players using special paraphernalia and wearing protective padding. The actual conduct of the game is not well understood, but is usually likened to modern soccer with the teams moving the ball down the court without using their hands and scoring goals at either end of the field. There was some connection between the game and human sacrifice, with the losers, or perhaps the winners, rewarded by meeting the gods.

Ball game paraphernalia is probably represented by the stone "yokes," "palmas" and "hachas" which are found at Veracruz sites. These elaborately carved ceremonial stones may represent the similarly shaped objects being used by the ball players depicted in relief carvings. For actual ball playing wooden equipment was more likely to have sufficed.

The activity, innovation and advances of the emerging Classic civilizations had only slight effect on the farmers and fishermen of Western Mexico. These were a conservative people and continued their Preclassic artistic traditions in ceramics throughout the Classic era with little concern for the development of monumental architecture, stone sculpture and other more elaborate modes of aesthetic expression. The peoples of Western Mexico were deeply involved with ritual for the dead. In the Jalisco-Colima area, shaft tombs were dug into the earth and furnished with pottery and ceramic replicas of things needed in the after life. Most well known are the Colima figures of the little hairless dog (an animal used for food), smoothly finished, slipped in bright red and modelled into a variety of appealing, lively poses. Clay representations of animals, birds, plants, sea shells, fish, and human figures were also included in the tombs. Men and women are seen standing, playing, drinking, and carrying heavy loads; warriors appear in aggressive poses while the afflictions of the more unfortunate members of this society—hunchbacks, dwarfs and persons with hideous diseases—were rendered with gross distortion.

THE POSTCLASSIC PERIOD   The end of the Classic Period was foretold by the fall of Teotihuacán. Teotihuacán was destroyed about 600 A.D. and its elegant central core was burned and sacked, possibly by rebellious elements among its own citizenry. In the following centuries, movements of displaced peoples and the influx of new groups into central Mexico caused dislocation

INTERIOR OF PALACE AT MITLA. Oaxaca, Mexico.
Post Classic. Photo by J. P. Dwyer.

and strife as far south as Guatemala. While it is now apparent that the early
stages of the Postclassic were marked by growing militarism, political disruption and changes in settlement patterns, no single area was able to assume
leadership. Many small but important centers seem to have been maintained
in all parts of Mesoamerica with the exception of the southern lowlands
where Classic Mayan culture became extinct. Finally, with the founding of
the Toltec capital at Tula in the modern state of Hidalgo around the tenth
century, central Mexico once again assumed the position of the dynamic
force in Mesoamerican politics. Significantly, this time also marks the emergence of the Mixtecs as a power in the southern Mexican highlands. The
ascendancy of Toltec and Mixtec power set the pattern for this new era and
defined a way of life which was to endure until the arrival of the Spanish in
1519.

The story of the Postclassic is one of great political, religious and probably social change. Militarism and warfare became the dominant modes of
action, and the followers of the gods of violence became prominent. According to Post Classic oral tradition, soon after the founding of Toltec Tula
conflict developed between the priests and followers of the peaceful god
Quetzalcóatl (the feathered serpent) and adherents of Tezcatlipoca, the god
of war and death. Quetzalcóatl was driven east and south to the Gulf Coast
leaving only a promise that he would return.

The site of Tula lies north of the Valley of Mexico. It is a large, pre-
sumably urban, center in an easily defensible location, but as yet there has
not been enough excavation of Tula to indicate more than the nature of its
largest structures. The main plaza is flanked by platform mounds supporting

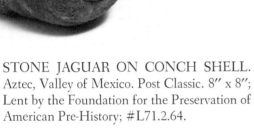

VOLCANIC STONE HEAD.
Toltec, Hidalgo, Mexico. Post
Classic. 17″ x 12″; Lent anony-
mously, 1911; #4738L.

STONE JAGUAR ON CONCH SHELL.
Aztec, Valley of Mexico. Post Classic. 8″ x 8″;
Lent by the Foundation for the Preservation of
American Pre-History; #L71.2.64.

large temples. Most impressive are large stone carvings as, for example, the columns in the form of warrior figures used to support the temple roof, the carved "Atlantean" figures of priests and the reclining "Chac Mool" figures with altars on their stomachs. The ceramic art of Tula consists of red on buff pottery wares featuring parallel wavy-line designs on bowl interiors, called Mazapán.

Influence from Tula can be seen in the architecture and the art of the Postclassic Maya of the Yucatan, especially at the site of Chichén Itzá. While all of the Maya centers of the southern Mesoamerican lowlands were abandoned by about 900 A.D., the Yucatan sites seem to have been successfully invaded by Mexican Toltecs and to have continued under the Toltec-Maya through the thirteenth century. The late architecture of Chichén Itzá is so similar to that of Tula that some archaeologists have accepted the myth of Quetzalcóatl's banishment from Tula as the description of an actual migration of Toltecs to the Yucatan.

Toltec power in central Mexico also declined with the destruction of Tula at the end of the twelfth century. It is at this point that the archaeology of central Mexico can be documented by native historical texts. Among numerous tribes of northerners who entered the Valley of Mexico at this time, the Aztecs became the center of recorded history. First serving as a military force allied to the various, more civilized city-states of the valley, they eventually became dominant and finally expanded their power far beyond central Mexico. Although states such as those of the Mixtecs and even the nearby

Tlaxcalans were never subsumed into an Aztec governmental system, they all feared and owed both allegiance and tribute to the Aztec ruler in his capital at Tenochtitlán.

Aztec art can only be described as awesome. The general purpose of all Postclassic artistic endeavor was to emphasize and disseminate the meaning of politico-religious institutions, and Aztec institutions were truly fearsome. The purpose of some works is clear within the context of Aztec ritual: elaborate vessels, for example, known as *cuauhxicalli* or "eagle vases" in honor of the Eagle Knights whose mission it was to secure victims for sacrifice, were receptacles for still beating human hearts. Sculpture and painting often depict scenes of sacrifice and death or of the gods who feed on the hearts and the blood of men.

Important prestige materials for art were jade and turquoise, obsidian, feathers, and, of course, gold. It was this metal, so valued in Europe, that attracted the Spanish to the Aztec capital. Montezuma's first gift to Cortés consisted of ornamented discs representing the sun and moon, one of gold "as big as a cartwheel" and the other—even larger—of silver, "twenty golden ducks and dogs, many articles of gold worked in the shape of tigers, lions and monkeys; collars beautifully wrought and other necklaces; arrows and a bow with its string and rods like staffs of justice . . . all in beautiful gold."

And so it was that lust for this metal drove the Spanish on to sack the city of Tenochtitlán, to destroy the government and empire of the Aztecs and to ravage the countryside of Mexico ending forever the process of independent high civilization and culture growth in that part of the world.

METATE (GRINDING STONE). Linea Vieja, Highland Region, Costa Rica. Late Classic. 5½″ x 8⅜″; Gift of the de Young Endowment; #42.13.

TRIPOD VESSEL WITH OWLS. Highland Region, Costa Rica. Post Classic. 6½″ x 5″; Gift of Mr. and Mrs. Joseph Bransten; #71.18.

Colombia, Panama and Costa Rica

In 1502, on his fourth and last journey to the New World, Columbus navagated along the shores of Central America and cast anchor off the coast of Panama. In his famous "Letters to the King and Queen of Spain," the Admiral—exhausted by the storms and sickness which plagued his expedition from the start—described this newly discovered land as a paradise "of lofty green mountains, fresh rivers and splendid forests." He was greatly impressed with its dense population and cultivated fields, but even more so by the golden ornaments worn by the Indians and their extravagant tales of rich mines of the precious metal.

Among the preconquest cultures of Colombia, Panama and Costa Rica, gold was the medium in which the artists best depicted the realm of the supernatural and the fantastic, monstrous creatures involved with their religious beliefs. Eagle beings with flat, spread wings, curved beaks, protruding eyes and claws are a very common motif, varied in many different ways by anthropormorphization or by combination with the features of monkeys, serpents, and jaguars. Many other monster beings were depicted with two heads, appearing to represent a significant mythological motif or religious concept. Golden figures of supernatural warriors, animals and birds were joined in single pendants, linked together by rods, by intertwined appendages and serpent figures or by a frame encircling all or part of the design.

Gold working seems to have been first practiced in Peru and then spread to Colombia and Costa Rica. The metal was panned in rivers or collected as nuggets, and then worked in a wide variety of complex processes. Large breast plates, collars and bands were hammered, then placed over some soft metal so that designs could be impressed with an awl, a technique known as repoussé. Hammering hardens gold and the Indian goldsmith would anneal or soften it by heat to make it workable again. Small wooden or copal carvings were sheathed in gold sheets while pieces of the metal were crimped by folding into place. Separate objects were often soldered together by tie rods. Casting was the most difficult technique and required considerable skill. Early attempts made use of solid casting methods; the molten metal was poured into a two-piece clay mold and allowed to harden. Hollow casting was even more complex and many unusual forms—even figures with articulated movable parts were made. Using the lost wax method the goldworker first shaped the core in a charcoal and clay mixture. This was then covered with a coating of wax which was modeled to the exact shape desired and finally this wax model was further encased with the charcoal and clay mixture. Pegs or chaplets were set through the mold to keep the core from slipping and vents provided. When the mold dried, the wax was melted out through the vents, leaving a hollow space into which the molten gold was poured. Tumbaga, the gold-copper alloy, was often used for these ornaments. After casting, an object made of tumbaga was treated by a process known as "mise en couleur"—an acid bath followed by burnishing—which removed the copper from its surface.

A number of graves in Panama and Costa Rica have yielded objects which evidence the custom of "killing" or deliberate breaking of these offerings before they were buried, and many fine golden ornaments have been found bent and smashed. In some cases this jewelry was never completely finished and never worn, but appears to have been created hurriedly and specifically as funeral offerings.

Archaeological sites throughout the region are exceptionally rich in stone sculpture and pottery as well as gold ornaments. Volcanic stone was carved in a monumental scale into male and female figures, some carrying severed heads or sacrificial knives; other sculptures represent merely the severed trophy head alone, showing its importance as a war and cult object. There are strange and grotesque monster deities in stone as well, appearing in the form of alligator-headed human figures, eagles and other birds, fanged felines and monkey-like creatures. These same mythical motifs were used as three-dimensional ornamentation on ceremonial *metates* or grinding stones and stools. Small pieces of colorful stone as well as shell, copal, whale tooth ivory and other unusual materials were worked into the form of miniature figures, beads and effigy pendants.

MEXICO

GUATEMALA

BRITISH HONDURAS

HONDURAS

EL SALVADOR

NICARAGUA

Caribbean Sea

COSTA
RICA

Linea Vieja

Peninsula de Nicoya

Disquís

Chiriqui

P A N A M A

Coclé

Sinú

Tairona

VENEZUELA

Pacific Ocean

COLOMBIA

100 50 0   100   200   300 300

STATUTE MILES

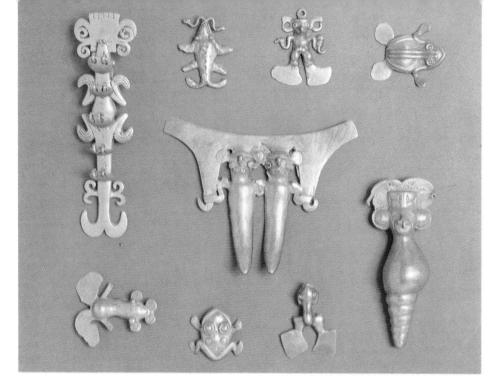

CAST GOLD ORNAMENTS. Costa Rica, Panama and Colombia. de Young Museum Endowment Fund, 1927; clockwise from top left: 2″ x 1⅝″, #53658; 1⅞″ x 1½″, #53661; 1¾″ x 1⅜″, #53660; 5⅝″ x 1½″, #53645; 2¼″ x 2″, #53656; 1⅜″ x 1⅜″, #53659; 1¾″ x 1″, #53657; 4¼″ x 1¾″, #53487; center 4″ x 5″, #53641.

BIRD EFFIGY VESSEL. Zapatero Island, Nicaragua. Late Classic. 9⅛″ x 22½″; Gift of Mr. Joseph Coney, #59.37.

Central Andes

The Central Andes, including Peru and parts of adjacent Bolivia, is a land of awesome environmental contrasts. Its coastal plain is desert, relatively narrow in the north but broadening in the south to a wilderness of shifting sand dunes and barren hills. Here, almost any form of human habitation would be impossible without the intermittent rivers which flow down from the highlands, across the coastal plain to empty into the Pacific Ocean. These rivers create narrow belts of vegetation—the fertile river valleys along which a number of the important Precolumbian civilizations of the Central Andes flourished. Beyond the coastal plain, the snow-capped peaks of the Andes rise to elevations of over 23,000 feet. Along these mountain ranges there are valleys, basins and high plains or "punas" which were occupied from the time of man's earliest migrations into South America. To the east of the mountains, where the Andes slope abruptly down into the tropical Amazon Basin, is the warm, humid Montaña, an area covered with lush jungle vegetation.

Because of the differences in the conditions for preservation of ancient artifacts, as well as differences in working conditions for the modern-day archaeologist, we know a good deal about the prehistory of the coastal regions, less about the highlands, and relatively little about the tropical forest. Nevertheless, it is becoming increasingly clear that the ancient peoples of the tropical forest must have played major roles in the culture history of the total Central Andean area.

The story of the distinct Precolumbian cultures of the Central Andes is a long and a complex one. It begins with the small primitive bands of hunters who followed herds of game through the highland basins in the closing centuries of the glacial era and ends with the Spanish conquest of the Inca empire in 1535. It is convenient to divide this time span into a series of named periods, the earliest of which is called the Preceramic. During this time, the idea of cultivation and domestication of various edible and other useful plants spread throughout the area. Population seems to have increased and by approximately 2000 B.C. there were coastal centers where people worked at both farming and fishing. In some of these coastal communities, large temple-like structures and other public forms of architecture were built, perhaps at the command of religious or civic leaders.

The art of these Preceramic peoples has come down to us only on fragments of cloth, wood, gourds, and pieces of unbaked clay. Primary motifs were raptorial birds, various sea creatures, and, of course, the human figure.

Possibly other themes of importance existed, but evidence for them has not yet turned up in excavations of the large, sooty middens or refuse mounds along the coast—the ruins of these once flourishing communities.

INITIAL PERIOD   The first appearance of pottery on the south coast of Peru marks the beginning of the Initial Period. Pottery manufacture was perhaps influenced by ideas which filtered south from Colombia or Ecuador, or even from the eastern jungles—all areas of possible earlier ceramic production. Although it added an extremely important new art medium, the earliest pottery was finely made but usually simple, without much decoration other than geometric patterns incised or painted on the surface. Such designs appear to have been patterning or decorative ornamentation without the complex iconographic base of religious, mythical or other meaningful depiction which characterizes the ceramic art of many of the cultures of succeeding epochs. By the end of the Initial Period, agriculture, herding, weaving and pottery, art and architecture, and urban living were present and formed the foundations upon which the later sophisticated civilizations of the Central Andes were to rest.

EARLY HORIZON   About 1200 B.C., perhaps earlier, art styles, as seen in pottery as well as in many other media, began to change and to reflect what was most likely the effect of a religious cult which had begun to spread over many areas of Peru. The origins of the new cult are as yet unknown. Some scholars feel it began on the north coast, others in the rain forests of the east-

PRECERAMIC AND INITIAL PERIOD CITY, LAS HALDAS. North Central Coast, Peru. Photo by E. B. Dwyer.

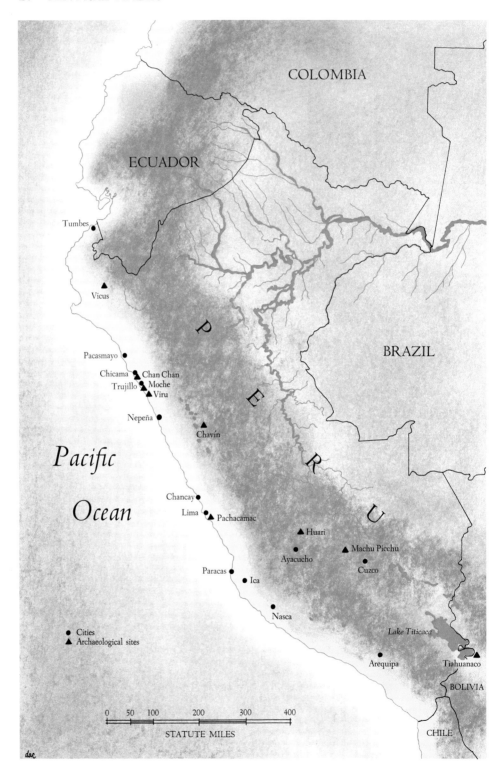

COLOMBIA

ECUADOR

BRAZIL

P

E

R

U

Tumbes

Vicus

Pacasmayo

Chicama

Chan Chan

Trujillo

Moche

Viru

Nepeña

Chavín

Pacific

Ocean

Chancay

Lima

Pachacamac

Huari

Ayacucho

Machu Picchu

Cuzco

Paracas

Ica

Nasca

● Cities
▲ Archaeological sites

Lake Titicaca

Arequipa

Tiahuanaco

BOLIVIA

CHILE

| 0 | 50 | 100 | 200 | 300 | 400 |

STATUTE MILES

dac

ern side of the Andes. However, the most imposing manifestation of the cult is found in the north central highlands of Peru at Chavín de Huántar, the elaborate temple city after which the cult and the culture of the people who spread it are named. The arrival of Chavín influence on the south coast of Peru begins the Early Horizon, a time when major areas of the Central Andes were united, perhaps not politically but through the force of a powerful religious ideology.

Chavín de Huántar was built in a quiet highland valley along the banks of a tributary of the great Marañon river facing the eastern slopes of the Andes. Even today the ruins of Chavín are very impressive. A wide sunken plaza stands before the facade of the largest temple, and an elaborately carved portal marks the stairway from the plaza to the top of the structure. The interiors of the temple platforms are honeycombed with carefully ventilated networks of passageways, stairs and galleries. Within the deep recesses of one building, excavators found a huge upright stone with its surfaces finely carved in relief to resemble an enormous human-like creature with snakes for hair and a smiling fanged mouth. This figure has been called the Smiling God and may be the oldest deity worshipped by the members of the Chavín cult.

Two other creatures, a mythical cayman and a fanged human figure shown front face and holding a staff in each hand, may have also been important Chavín deities. Both are found on carved stones which were placed within the temple structures in such a way as to suggest they held special places in the Chavín religious pantheon.

The strength of Chavín influence in widely separated areas is reflected by similarities in artistic style. On the north coast, the Cupisnique and Tembladera style ceramics were heavily and elegantly modelled into life forms— plants and animals, houses, grotesque human figures—or were strongly incised and textured, often with the coiling intricate motif of the fanged feline, using artistic conventions identical to those found on stone carvings at Chavín. Beginning a convention which was to endure even until Post Conquest times, these early north coastal vessels are characteristically a monochromatic black or grey, sometimes enlivened with a deep red or brown. They often have heavy stirrup-shaped spouts on top of oval chambers, a vessel shape which becomes a north coast tradition.

On the Peruvian south coast, involvement with the cult of Chavín appears to have been quite profound, although artistic expression was clearly modified by local taste and style. Among these modifications was a focus on color and two dimensionality, two qualities emphasized at least in the ceramics of this region. Until the final centuries of the Early Horizon there are close although varying correspondences in motif with those developed at Chavín. The feline, human figure, bird, and serpent-like motif are all important elements of the art of the south coast which are seen in the stone sculpture at Chavín. They may be combined into representations of what may have been the major deities and these different motifs continue through time as basic themes in much of the art of ancient Peru.

EARLY INTERMEDIATE PERIOD   With the decline of Chavín influence and the abandonment of the site of Chavín itself, there followed a period of regionalization within the areas once dominated by Chavín. Differences not only in art and architectural styles, but in settlement patterns, and possibly in government and religion became pronounced from valley to valley. During this epoch, known as the Early Intermediate Period, artists and craftsmen became specialists in certain media, and, experimenting with different methods and materials, they developed new technologies to profoundly enrich their art. A method for slip decoration of pottery, for example, replaced earlier post fired resin paints. Metallurgy took on added significance as methods for casting and alloying in gold and other metals were developed. A busy, far-flung trade was carried on in ordinary produce as well as in exotic materials. Colorful tropical shells, diverse semi-precious stones and other materials became available for the craftsman's use.

The tendency toward cultural diversity on the north coast was interrupted by the formation of an aggressive conquest state centered in the Moche, Chicama and Pacasmayo valleys.

These Moche people represent the florescence of north coast culture. Their ceremonial pottery is fine, thin walled, and shaped into bowls, flasks, and even more commonly, into spherical, flat bottomed vessels with stirrup spouts. Two-piece pottery molds were often used to produce the basic forms although the potter was also highly adept at free hand modelling. Designs were painted on each vessel with a simple two-color combination of red and white slip. Technically Moche pottery is of the highest quality; artistically it is unsurpassed for its naturalism and expressiveness.

Moche ceramic art has been divided into five chronological phases on the basis of changes in vessel form and painting style. This chronological control allows some statements about the expansion of the state and the conquest of valleys further north and south from Moche. The greatest expansion was accomplished by phase four of the stylistic sequence, perhaps around 400 A.D.

BLACK AND WHITE PORTAL, EARLY HORIZON
CEREMONIAL CENTER CHAVIN DE HUANTAR.
North Highlands, Peru. Photo by E. B. Dwyer.

At this time there were Moche sites all the way from the Jequetepeque Valley
in the north to the Nepeña Valley in the south.

The formation of the Moche state was not the only important event to
occur during the Early Intermediate Period. It was balanced by a tremendous
burst of artistic activity, very likely connected with religious revival, which
spread over the south coast. Beginning with the depiction of what appears to
be new deity figures in the art of Paracas during the last part of the Early
Horizon, south coast artists turned their attention to the polychrome depiction
of mythical creatures on both textiles and pottery.

Prominent at this time on the south coast was the colorful, symbolic art
style of the Paracas and Nasca peoples who developed a new religious symbolism in their ceramic and textile arts. Perhaps the advent of new cult practices and the breaking away from older traditional ritual modes brought strife
to the area, for the large south coastal cities of this time were strongly fortified
against invasion. Shrines, stepped adobe pyramids, plazas, and cemeteries
evidence a new sort of religious orientation which brought ever greater emphasis on the cult of the dead. For prominent individuals in south coast society, funerary offerings became richer than before: the deceased were given
offerings of brightly painted pottery vessels, their bodies were bejewelled with
gold and shell ornaments, then clothed in ponchos, shirts, turbans and other
garments and wrapped in shrouds to form a bundle. All of the textiles wrapping the body were laboriously prepared before death, and were ornately

patterned either while on the loom or by embroidery in an extraordinary range of motifs consisting of both mythological and naturalistic creatures.

The Occulate Being—a strange supernatural figure with large staring eyes and long nose first appears at this time, and figures prominently with other winged and masked figures, typically encumbered with trophy heads and protruding snake-like or tongue-like appendages. The more ancient feline motif emerges as a smiling cat, often amusingly intertwined with others or within the body of another larger cat. Handsomely drawn birds, fish and other animals and plants also appear in a multitude of vivid colors, and, along with mythological motifs, are, at first, easily recognizable although stylized. In the later phases of the Nasca style, both textile and the similar pottery motifs become increasingly conventionalized and abstract, complex and florid.

MIDDLE HORIZON About the 6th century A.D. significant changes began to occur throughout Peru. These events which had so profound an effect on the course of ancient Andean cultural history began gradually toward the end of the Early Intermediate Period when a growing restlessness is evident in more frequent conquest, migration and the lessening quality of artistic endeavor. The key area for these extraordinary developments was the south and central regions of the coast and highlands. Here, enormous urban settlements had

STIRRUP SPOUT VESSEL. Paracas style, South Coast, Peru. Early Horizon. 7½″ x 4″; Lent anonymously; #L71.14.-18.

VESSEL WITH MODELED CRAYFISH. Moche style, North Coast, Peru. Early Intermediate Period. 9″ x 6½″; Gift of the Henry Crocker Estate; #61.1.22.

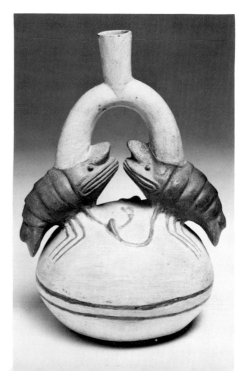

STIRRUP SPOUT VESSEL. Moche style, North Coast, Peru. Early Intermediate Period. 8⅛″ x 5¾″; Gift of the Henry Crocker Estate; #61.1.22.

TEMPLE FACADE, CERRO SECHIN. North Coast, Peru. Late Early Horizon. Photo by E. B. Dwyer.

STIRRUP SPOUT VESSEL WITH
HUNTING SCENE. Moche style, North
Coast, Peru. Early Intermediate Period. 12″ x
6″; Gift of Arthur M. Scully, Jr.; #61.1.12.

STIRRUP SPOUT VESSEL OF KNEEL-
ING WARRIOR. Moche style, North Coast,
Peru. Early Intermediate Period. 7¼″ x 4½″;
Gift of the Henry Crocker Estate; #61.1.9.

grown up in the previous centuries. Tiahuanaco in Bolivia, Huari north of
Ayacucho, a number of other cities around Ayacucho itself and Nasca on the
coast are all linked to the powerful religious and political movements which
ushered in the next chronological period—the Middle Horizon.

The beginning of this significant epoch is marked by rapidly shifting
centers of power and spheres of influence in which the cities of Tiahuanaco
and Huari ultimately prevailed. Tiahuanaco was a magnificent ceremonial
center built on the high, bleak and windswept plain on the east side of Lake
Titicaca. Its ruins, although not yet totally explored, consist of stone pyramids, platforms and plazas, subterranean chambers, massive stone figures and
carved pillars.

The iconography of this time period, at first restricted to purely ceremonial objects, seems to reveal yet another religious movement or cult which
spread rapidly throughout the highland area. A prominent figure depicted
holding a staff in each hand may indicate a revival of some part of the ancient
Chavín cult. Pilgrims or missionaries carried the word of the new cult in the
early years of the Middle Horizon but, as it gradually became an established
religion, political and military power apparently became an important factor
in its dissemination. Tiahuanaco and its companion city, Huari, further north,

BIRD EFFIGY BOTTLE. Nasca, South Coast, Peru. Early Intermediate Period. 6¾″ x 3¾″; Lent by Mrs. Alan Lowry; #L71.27.1.

DOUBLE SPOUT AND BRIDGE VESSEL DEPICTING MYTHICAL BIRD. Nasca, South Coast, Peru. Early Intermediate Period. 8½″ x 6½″; Gift of the Henry Crocker Estate; #61.1.7.

EMBROIDERED TEXTILE BAND. Paracas Necropolis, South Coast, Peru. Early Intermediate Period. 16½″ x 3¾″; 20½″ x 3¼″; de Young Endowment, 1934; #54527B, 54528.

JAR WITH MAN HOLDING A WHISTLE. Nasca, South Coast, Peru. Early Intermediate Period. 9¼″ x 5¾″; de Young Endowment, 1934; #54519.

became strong, yet separate, political powers—perhaps even empires—extending their influence north, south and westward to the coast. As this occurred, art motifs became increasingly secularized and were no longer solely restricted to religious architectural decoration and ritual paraphernalia—perhaps reflecting the rise of an elite class who utilized the symbols of religion to emphasize personal status.

Although its motifs on textiles, ceramics, featherwork, metal and other elegant artistic products were curiously limited in their variety, the new art flourished everywhere and for several centuries completely effaced the older styles of the previous period. Tapestries, which have been best preserved along the south and central coast, show the winged staff-bearing figures, trophy and feline heads and other elements of this iconography. Colors are exceptionally brilliant and although the majority of textiles were executed in fine tapestry weaves, other richly decorative techniques such as knotted pile cloth and tie dyeing are found. Pottery also underwent an extraordinary transformation in every area of Tiahuanaco-Huari influence, and earlier forms were replaced with such characteristic Middle Horizon shapes as the straight and flairing sided tumblers, flasks, bottles and a simple, squat, double-spouted jar with bridge handle.

CEREMONIAL AND STORAGE CENTER, PIKILLACTA.
Southern Highlands, Peru. Aerial view courtesy of Servicio Aerofotografía Nacional, Lima.

DOUBLE SPOUT AND BRIDGE VESSEL SHOWING GRIFFIN. Pachacamac style, Central Coast, Peru. Middle Horizon. 6" x 8¼"; Gift of Mrs. Herbert Fleishhacker; #52.39.39.

The end of the Middle Horizon was marked by the fall of the Tiahuanaco and Huari empires and the end of highland political and religious influence over the entire central Andean region. For reasons yet unknown, by about 800 A.D. the great highland cities were abandoned and the prestige, wealth and population of the south and central coastal settlements had declined. The art of the coastal regions never regained its former splendor even though in certain areas there was an attempt to revert back to the ancient styles of the Early Intermediate Period.

LATE INTERMEDIATE PERIOD   The Late Intermediate Period reflects the artistic regionalism and political fractioning present before Middle Horizon times. In the south, the peoples of the Ica Valley built large and imposing

EFFIGY HEAD TUMBLERS. Chancay Valley, Central Coast, Peru. Middle Horizon. 5" x 5"; Lent Anonymously; #L71.14.14/15.

STANDING FIGURE. Chimu-Inca style, Chancay Valley, Central Coast, Peru. Late Horizon. 10½″ x 4⅛″; Gift of Mrs. Herbert Fleishhacker; #52.39.50.

MONKEY EFFIGY. Chancay style, Central Coast, Peru. Late Intermediate Period. 11¼″ x 5¾″; Gift of Mrs. Herbert Fleishhacker; #52.39.1.

ceremonial centers and developed new ceramic and textile styles based on small geometric units such as zigzags, crosses, step frets, as well as some highly conventionalized life forms. The Chancay ceramic style of the central coast is technically less impressive but its style of black and white painting is highly decorative and its motifs of monkeys, whimsical felines and human figures are appealing. Textiles are of brightly colored cotton, wool or both, patterned with conventionalized birds, fish, felines or geometric designs and intricately woven into gauzes, double cloth and tapestries.

Far more is known of north coastal civilizations of this time, especially the Kingdom of Chimor, whose oral tradition of important events, ruling dynasties and mythology was in part preserved to historic times. Beginning in the mid-14th century A.D. the Chimu kings of Chimor embarked on an ambitious program of conquest which eventually made them rulers of a vast empire extending from Tumbes on the present northern border of Peru south to perhaps the Chancay or Chillon valleys on the north central coast.

Like the much earlier Moche, the Chimu kings surrounded themselves with luxury, pomp and ceremony, and with an enormous retinue of courtiers and servants. Their capital was established at Chan Chan, a strange and magnificent city where mud brick ruins are still imposing today. Within its

VESSEL SHOWING COUPLE ON BALSA. Chimu style, North Coast, Peru. Late Intermediate Period. 6″ x 6½″; Gift of Mr. Drew Childester, 1931; #53756A.

STIRRUP SPOUT VESSEL SHOWING DEITY ON BALSA. Moche style, North Coast, Peru. Early Intermediate Period. 10½″ x 4¼″; Gift of the Henry Crocker Estate; #61.1.56.

INCA PALACE AT PISAC. Southern Highlands, Peru. Late Horizon. Photo by E. B. Dwyer.

limits are compounds with walls standing as much as 30 to 40 feet high constructed of adobe bricks covered with a clay plaster. The plaster was often cut out over much of the building's surface to form raised designs reminiscent of textile patterns—scrolls, diamonds, frets, birds, snake-like figures and stylized animals.

The historical chronicles also reveal some few aspects of Chimu religion perhaps reflecting the continuity of even more ancient north coastal beliefs. The powerful Moon Goddess, stars and other celestial deities, charged with maintaining the regularity of the weather and fertility of the fields, were of prime importance as was the sea, which provided food and other necessary products. Ancestor worship appears to have continued as the basis for a cult of the dead, and burials of high ranking individuals were of incomparable richness, particularly in luxury objects of gold and silver.

Metallurgy attained an exceptional degree of elegance and technological accomplishment among the Chimu. In fact, with a few exceptions, they mastered most of the techniques used in metal-working today. Gold, silver, copper, tin, and lead were hammered, decorated with repoussé or raised designs, and inlaid with turquoise and other colorful stones to make mummy masks, ceremonial and funerary vessels, jewelry and a host of other objects. Fine casting in the lost wax method, or with open and closed molds, produced objects of great intricacy. Annealing, soldering, plating, alloying and gilding were all expertly practiced.

INCA TAPESTRY. Peru. Colonial Period. 34¾" x 23½";
Gift of Miss Else Shilling; #59.5.1.

While the Chimu excelled in these luxury items, possibly in response to the desire of the ruling classes for lavish symbols of power and status, the very ancient forms of ceremonial arts, textiles and pottery, never reached the level they had attained before Middle Horizon times. Textiles are similar to those of other coastal regions but Chimu pottery is highly distinctive. There was evidently an attempt to revitalize the ancient Moche styles in particular motifs as well as such forms as the stirrup spout and the use of molds and pressed relief designs. A certain realism returned to the art style and animals, vegetables, and other common objects, human and deity figures were all portrayed, generally in a highly polished black or more rarely red ware.

While the Chimu state on the north coast was growing and consolidating its territory, there was considerable political turmoil in other parts of the Central Andes. One of the groups competing for power and prestige was to become remarkably successful.

The Inca shrouded their origins in myth. It is known that they were only one of a number of diverse groups vying for power in the central and southern highlands during the Late Intermediate Period. The rise of the Inca in a single century from a relatively insignificant people to the rulers of a vast empire which stretched from Chile to Ecuador is the last and one of the most remarkable episodes in Central Andean prehistory. Legends tell of the first king, or Inca, named Manco Capac who was guided by divine providence to choose the site of Cuzco where he founded the first Inca capital.

SILVER TUMBLER. Huarmey Valley, Central Coast, Peru. Late Horizon. 4″ x 3⅝″; de Young Endowment, 1936; #54897.

WHISTLING JAR. Chimu-Inca style, Chancay Valley, Central Coast, Peru. (Said to have been found together with standing figure; #52.39.50.) Late Horizon. 6″ x 4¼″; Gift of Mrs. Herbert Fleishhacker; #52.39.51.

Through a series of military victories and alliances, later Inca rulers subdued the various tribes surrounding them and became a significant power. However, it was not until the reign of the famed Pachacuti Inca Yupanki—from 1438 to 1471—that conquest began in earnest and Inca power was gradually extended toward the eastern slopes of the Andes, westward to the coast, along the northern highlands and finally into the rich kingdom of Chimor.

With the rapid growth of the empire, Pachacuti and his successor Topa Inca were faced with immense problems in administering and maintaining control of these endless domains. With extraordinary genius, they devised a new state religion emphasizing a single creator god whose power was represented in the Emperor, appointed a hierarchy of priests and officials to carry out the rituals of the new religion and to insure that government edicts were obeyed (they instituted the concept of religious confession of sins), built roads and set up modes of communication between distant parts of the empire. They also rebuilt Cuzco to give it the prestige of an imperial capital.

As the empire expanded further, fortresses, government centers, warehouses, palaces and temples arose in strategic locations. This architecture in its austerity, awesome monumentality and ingenious construction reflects the practical and intelligent nature of the Inca themselves. The fortresses of Sacsayhuaman and Ollantaytambo in the Cuzco region, for example, are remarkable and handsome structures built of massive stone blocks carefully fitted together. Other structures were built with smaller rectangular blocks, often beautifully cut with sunken joints and placed in regular courses.

As befitted their status, the Inca nobility enjoyed all the luxuries their empire could provide. Gold symbolized the sun and was strictly reserved for the use of the emperor. The Spanish Conquerors who entered Cuzco in 1533 were astounded at the incredible riches of jewelry, vessels and all types of sculpture made of precious metals which they found in the palaces of the Emperor and his enshrined ancestors. Ceremonial buildings such as the great Temple of the Sun were equally splendid. Spanish accounts tell us that doors and gateways of the temple were sheathed in gold, and in one part of the enclosure stood a golden image of the Sun, its circumference prolonged by rays and flames so immense that it occupied the entire wall of the temple.

The Inca did not carry on the highland tradition of massive free standing stone sculpture developed by the artists of Chavín and Tiahuanaco. Large natural rock outcroppings in the vicinity of Cuzco are nearly all carved with geometric and naturalistic forms, but the significance of this carving within Inca culture is not known. Smaller sculptures in metal and stone were preva-

FEATHER BIRD. Ica Valley, South Coast, Peru. Late Horizon. 8″ x 4″; de Young Art Trust; #72.3.4.

lent. Tiny figures of humans and animals, especially llamas and alpacas, were carved in stone, or cast in bronze, silver or gold. These small pieces were used in making offerings and many of them have been preserved until today. Unfortunately, the larger metal objects described in the Spanish Chronicles did not survive the looting which took place at the time of the Conquest. They were all melted down for easy division among the conquering horde.

The Inca nobility were accustomed to the use of gold and silver vessels but the common people used pottery, typically of excellent manufacture and simply yet elegantly shaped and decorated. The storage jar or aryballus is distinctive of Inca ceramic wares as are the pedestal bowls and the flat dish with tiny lugs or knobs. Inca ceramics—like much of their other arts—were functional and painted with restrained colors and geometric designs. Perhaps much of the Inca pottery seems so standardized because what has come down to us was mainly army or state utensils. Textiles, featherwork and wooden objects which show strong Inca influence have been best preserved in coastal areas. Textiles, especially indicative of this Late Horizon style, are strongly yet simply patterned with brightly colored bands along the hem, large areas of plain checkerboard or overall patterning of small squares or diamonds, each containing some geometric or conventionalized motif. The most typical wooden artifacts are straight-sided tumblers called Keros which are decorated with geometric carvings. Post conquest Keros are decorated with inlaid lacquer drawings of Inca life.

BIBLIOGRAPHY
A BRIEF LIST OF SOME BASIC WORKS

AFRICA

Allison, Phillip. *African Stone Sculpture*. New York: Frederick A. Praeger, 1968.

Bastin, Marie-Louise. *Art decoratif Tshokwe*. 2 vols. Lisbon: Companhia de Diamantes de Angola, 1961.

Biebuyck, Daniel, ed. *Tradition and Creativity in Tribal Art*. Berkeley and Los Angeles: University of California Press, 1969.

Bradbury, R. E. "The Benin Kingdom and the Edo-speaking Peoples of South-western Nigeria," *Ethnographic Survey of Africa*, 13 (1957).

Fraser, D. and H. M. Cole. *African Art and Leadership*. Madison: University of Wisconsin Press, 1972.

Harley, George W. "Notes on the Poro in Liberia." *Papers of the Peabody Museum of Archaeology and Ethnology, Harvard*, XIX, 2 (1941).

McCulloch, M., M. Littlewood, and I. Dugast. "Peoples of the Central Cameroons." *Ethnographic Survey of Africa*, 9 (1954).

Paques, Viviana. *Les Bambara*. Paris: Presses Universitaires de France, 1954.

Paulme, Denise. *Les gens du riz: Kissi de Haute-Guinée française*. Paris, 1954.

Rattray, Robert S. *Religion and Art in Ashanti*. Oxford: Clarendon Press, 1927.

Schwab, George. "Tribes of the Liberian Hinterland." *Papers of the Peabody Museum of Archaeology and Ethnology, Harvard*, 31 (1947).

de Sousberghe, L. *L'art Pende*. Gembloux: J. Duculot, S.A., 1958.

Starkweather, F. *Traditional Igbo Art: 1966*. Ann Arbor: University of Michigan Press, 1968.

Talbot, P. A. *The Peoples of Southern Nigeria*. 4 vols. London: Oxford University Press, 1926.

Tessman, G. *Die Pangwe*. Berlin: Ernst Wasmuth, 1913.

Torday, E. and T. A. Joyce. "Les Bushongo." *Annales du Musée du Congo Belge*, ser. 3, vol. 2, fasc. 1 (1910).

Thompson, Robert F. "Black Gods and Kings." *Occasional Papers of the Museum and Laboratories of Ethnic Arts and Technology, University of California, Los Angeles*, 2 (1971).

Willett, Frank. *Ife in the History of West African Sculpture*. London: Thames and Hudson, 1967.

OCEANIA

Archey, Gilbert. *South Sea Folk: Handbook of Maori and Oceanic Ethnology*. Auckland: Auckland War Memorial Museum, 1949.

Bateson, Gregory. *Naven*. London: Cambridge University Press, 1936.

Best, Elsdon. "The Maori." *Polynesian Society Memoir No. 5*, 2 vols. (1924).

Buck, Peter H. "Arts and Crafts of the Cook Islands." *Bernice P. Bishop Museum, Bulletin No. 179* (1944).

Codrington, R. H. *The Melanesians*. Oxford: Clarendon Press, 1891.

Deacon, A. B. *Malekula*. London: Routledge and Kegan Paul, 1934.

Firth, Raymond. *Art and Life in New Guinea*. London and New York: Studio Publications, 1936.

Gerbrands, Adrian. *Wow-Ipits*. The Hague and Paris: Mouton, 1967.

Handy, E. S. C. "Polynesian Religion." *Bernice P. Bishop Museum, Bulletin No. 34* (1927).

Kaberry, Phyllis M. "The Abelam Tribe, Sepik District, New Guinea." *Oceania*, 11 (1940–1941).

Lewis, Phillip H. "The Social Context of Art in Northern New Ireland." *Fieldiana: Anthropology*, 58 (1969).

Malinowski, Bronislaw. *Argonauts of the Western Pacific*. New York: E. P. Dutton, 1961.

Malo, David. "Hawaiian Antiquities." *Bernice P. Bishop Museum, Special Publication No. 2* (1951).

Métraux, Alfred. *Easter Island*. New York: Oxford University Press, 1957.

Powdermaker, Hortense. *Life in Lesu*. New York: W. W. Norton and Co., 1971.

von den Steinen, Karl. *Die Marquesaner und ihre Kunst*. 3 vols. Berlin: Reimer, 1925–1928.

NORTH AMERICA

Amsden, Charles A. *Navaho Weaving, Its Technique and History*. Santa Ana: Fine Arts Press, 1934.

Barbeau, Marius. "Totem Poles." *National Museum of Canada, Anthropological Series, 30, Bulletin 119*. 2 vols. (1950–1951).

———. "Haida Carvers." *National Museum of Canada, Anthropological Series 38, Bulletin 139* (1957).

Boas, Franz. "The Social Organization and Secret Societies of the Kwakiutl Indians." *United States National Museum, Annual Report* (1897).

Bunzel, Ruth L. "The Pueblo Potter." *Columbia University Contributions to Anthropology*, 8 (1929).

Curtis, Edward S. *The North American Indian*. 20 vols. Cambridge, 1907–1930.

Cushing, Frank H. "Zuñi Fetishes." *Bureau of American Ethnology, Annual Report*, 2 (1883), 9–45.

Krause, Aurel. "The Tlingit Indians." (Translated by Erna Gunther) *Memoirs of the American Ethnological Society*, 26 (1956).

Kroeber, Alfred L. "Handbook of the Indians of California." *Bureau of American Ethnology, Bulletin 78* (1925).

Lantis, Margaret. "Alaskan Eskimo Ceremonialism." *American Ethnological Society, Monograph 11* (1947).

Lowie, Robert H. *Indians of the Plains*. New York, 1954.

Mason, Otis T. "Aboriginal American Basketry." *United States National Museum, Annual Report*.

Mooney, James. *The Ghost Dance Religion and the Sioux Outbreak of 1890*. Chicago: University of Chicago Press, 1965.

Parsons, Elsie C. *Pueblo Indian Religion*. Chicago, 1930.

Ray, Dorothy J. *Eskimo Masks: Art and Ceremony*. Seattle: University of Washington Press, 1967.

Stevenson, Matilde C. "The Zuñi Indians: Their Mythology, Esoteric Societies and Ceremonies." *Bureau of American Ethnology, Annual Report* (1904).

Willey, Gordon R. *An Introduction to American Archaeology, Vol. 1: North and Middle America*. Englewood Cliffs: Prentice-Hall, 1966.

MESOAMERICA

Benson, Elizabeth P., *Dumbarton Oaks Conference on the Olmec*. Washington, D. C.: Trustees for Harvard University, 1968.

Drucker, Phillip, R. F. Heizer, and R. J. Squier. "Excavations at La Venta Tabasco, 1955." *Bureau of American Ethnology, Bulletin 170* (1959).

Jennings, J. D. and E. Norbeck, eds. *Prehistoric Man in the New World*. Chicago: University of Chicago Press, 1964.

Kidder, A. V., J. D. Jennings, and E. M. Shook. "Excavations at Kaminaljuyú, Guatemala." *Carnegie Institution of Washington, Publication 561* (1946).

Marquina, Ignacio. *Arquitectura Prehispánica*. Mexico: Instituto Nacionál de Antropología e Historia, 1951.

Medellin Zenil, Alfonso. *Cerámicas del Totonacapan*. Xalapa, Veracruz: Universidad Veracruzana, Instituto de Antropología, 1960.

Millon, R. F. "The Teotihuacán Mapping Project." *American Antiquity*, XXIX, 3 (1964), 345–352.

Paddock, John (ed). *Ancient Oaxaca*. Stanford: Stanford University Press, 1966.

Porter, M. N. "Tlatilco and the Pre-Classic Cultures of the New World." *Viking Fund Publications in Anthropology*, 19 (1956).

Proskouriakoff, Tatiana. "Varieties of Classic Central Veracruz Sculpture." *Contributions to American Anthropology and History*, 58, Publication 606 (1954), 61–121.

Wauchope, Robert, ed. *Handbook of Middle American Indians*. 12 vols. Austin: University of Texas Press, 1964–.

SOUTH AMERICA

Benson, Elizabeth P., ed. *Dumbarton Oaks Conference on Chavín.* Washington, D. C.: Trustees for Harvard University, 1971.

Cobo, Bernabé. "Obras del P. Bernabe Cobo." *Biblioteca de Antores Españoles,* 91–92 (1956).

Lanning, E. P. *Peru Before the Incas.* New Jersey: Prentice-Hall, Inc., Englewood Cliffs, 1967.

Menzel, Dorothy. "Style and Time in the Middle Horizon." *Nawpa Pacha* 2 (1964), 1–106.

Poma de Ayala, Felipe Guaman. "Nueva Corónica y Buen Gobierno (codex Peruvien Illustré)." *Travaux et Memoires,* 23 (1936).

Ponce Sangines, Carlos, ed. *Arqueología Boliviana.* La Paz: Biblioteca Pacena, 1957.

Posnansky, Arthur. *Tiahuanacu: The Cradle of American Man.* New York: J. J. Augustin, 1945.

Rowe, J. H. "The Kingdom of Chimor." *Acta Americana,* VI, 1–2 (1948).

————. "Form and Meaning in Chavín Art." *Peruvian Archaeology: Selected Readings,* edited by J. H. Rowe and Dorothy Menzel. Palo Alto: Peek Publications, 1968.

Steward, Julian H., ed. "Handbook of South American Indians, Vol. 2." *Bureau of American Ethnology Bulletin* 143 (1946).

Stone, D. Z. *Introduction to the Archaeology of Costa Rica.* San Jose, Costa Rica: Museo Nacionál, 1958.